Brief Lives:
Honoré de Balzac

Brief Lives:
Honoré de Balzac

David Carter

ET REMOTISSIMA PROPE

Brief Lives
Published by Hesperus Press Limited
4 Rickett Street, London sw6 1ru
www.hesperuspress.com

First published by Hesperus Press Limited, 2008

Designed and typeset by Fraser Muggeridge studio
Printed in Jordan by Jordan National Press

ISBN: 978-1-84391-908-7

Contents

Introduction

It would appear that he was constantly able to maintain a pace of life and work which would have shattered most ordinary mortals at a far younger age. That he made it to the age of fifty-one is itself a wonder. Honoré de Balzac, the self-styled aristocrat, drove himself mercilessly in pursuit of goals which he could never realistically achieve in their entirety. Yet how did a man who failed so disastrously in so many of his enterprises nevertheless manage to accomplish so much: a cycle of interrelated novels and stories which reflect a whole epoch of French society, but have fascinated readers the world over for the universality of their themes? The author himself clearly hoped for as much in calling his collected works 'The Human Comedy' (*La Comédie humaine*).

Speculation will doubtless never cease to seek and never discover a satisfactory explanation for the relentless driving force in Balzac's life. Can it all be traced to the deprivation of motherly love? Throughout his life there is evidence of a constant search for the one woman who would embody all his ideals and coincidentally solve all his problems: she should be motherly, mature, aristocratic in manner and in fortune (if possible), and admiring of his genius.

Another source of the powerful driving force in Balzac's life was the constant need to satisfy his creditors, and his motive for moving houses so often was precisely to avoid them. He developed countless hare-brained schemes to settle his debts once and for all, none of them ultimately successful, and always only putting off the day of final reckoning.

Before settling on prose fiction as his true métier, he also endeavoured to demonstrate his genius in other fields: in verse drama, prose drama, popular essays, journalism and publishing. In fact, until late in his life Balzac obviously hankered after success as a dramatist.

How did he manage it all? Certainly at the expense of his health, and with the aid of the many cups of coffee which have entered into the legends that surround him.

There were also many women in Balzac's life, some of whom he met after they wrote him admiring letters about his novels. There is also strong evidence, both from correspondence and from the novels, that many of Balzac's attachments to young men probably had a homosexual component.

Honoré de Balzac thus made of his life a narrative every bit as salacious, and, at times, improbable, as the heightened realism of his novels. There were definitely moments when he found it difficult to distinguish between the worlds he was creating for himself to live in and those he conjured up in his fiction.

Formative Years
1799–1819

Honoré de Balzac was born the second son of Bernard-François Balssa and Anne Charlotte-Laure née Sallambier, in the busy centre of the city of Tours in the Touraine region of France. To be precise this occurred at eleven o'clock, on 20th May 1799. Exactly one year before, on 20th May 1798, a first son, Louis-Daniel, had been born, but had lived for only thirty-three days. In September 1800, there followed a daughter, Laure, and it is assumed that the second daughter, Laurence, was born in 1802. A younger brother, Henry-François, was born in 1807. Despite Honoré's later modification of his name to 'Balzac' and his adoption of the would-be aristocratic 'de', he came, on his father's side, from a long line of peasants in southern France and, on his mother's side, from a family of haberdashers in the Marais district of Paris.

It is worth considering for a few moments the life of Honoré's father, for he was a person every bit as fascinating and remarkable as one of his son's own creations. Determined to rise above the station of peasant, he asked the parish priest to teach him to read and write. He then became a clerk in a lawyer's office, and eventually, before the age of twenty, went off to seek a career for himself in Paris. By the time he was thirty, he had served an apprenticeship as a clerk to the Public Prosecutor and become Secretary to the King's Council. During the Revolution, however, he became a member of the Commune, and during the

Terror he organised escapes for several of those who had formerly protected him. And it was probably Danton himself who saved Bernard-François from persecution by Robespierre by sending him up north in charge of food provisions to the army. With the same responsibilities he was transferred to Tours in 1795. He was invited to become mayor of the city but preferred to devote his energies to running the local hospital. He had several eccentric obsessions: he believed, for example, that he could live to the age of one hundred by breathing as much fresh air as possible, wearing only comfortable clothes and not yielding to sexual desire too frequently. He also invested in a unique early form of life insurance, known in French as a *tontine*. This was an arrangement whereby a group of people invested money together and the last surviving member inherited the lot. Fans of Agatha Christie will recognise this as a crucial element in the plot of the Miss Marple mystery *4.50 From Paddington*.

Much has been made of the fact that Honoré was not breast-fed by his mother but nursed by another woman away from his parental home. It seems likely that the reason for this was at least partly that his mother felt she had failed her first-born by trying to feed him herself. However it appears that it was fairly common in the years after the Revolution for mothers to send their children to wet-nurses. Writing later of that time, Balzac stated that 'ninety-nine per cent of mothers put their babies out to nurse'.[1] The decision was also clearly in accordance with his father's belief in the benefits of fresh air, as the house of the nurse was situated on the outskirts of the town where the air was cleaner. Honoré stayed there not just for the weaning period, however, but for the first four years of his life. The deprivation of motherly love in these early years clearly encourages psychoanalytic speculation about the effects on the boy's psychological development. Hard evidence for firm conclusions is, however, difficult to come by.

His sister, Laure, and in all likelihood Laurence too, eventually joined him at the nurse's home. The children were finally allowed to return to their parents' home in 1803. When his maternal grandfather died, his grandmother came to live with them to be near her daughter, and developed a close relationship with the children. However they also came under the influence of a formidable governess, Miss Caroline Delahaye, who required them to respect and obey her at all times. She was very much supported by the children's mother in this, while their father tended to believe it was more beneficial to let them follow their natural instincts.

In April 1804, Honoré was sent to the nearby Pension Le Guay as a day boy. The pupils there were mainly the sons of middle-class families and tradesmen. From his own later accounts of his period in this school it appears that his behaviour was rebellious at times and he was quite popular with the other boys. The school life depicted in the very autobiographical novel *Le Lys dans la Vallée* is based considerably on experiences in this school, and provides the main source of information on that stage of his education, for there are unfortunately no school reports available on him before 1807.

At the age of eight he was sent to the Collège de Vendôme, in the town of Vendôme, thirty-five miles north-east of Tours, and closer to Paris. He stayed there for the next ten years, during which time he saw his mother only twice. This was not entirely due to parental preference, because the school, considered one of the finest of its kind in France, also insisted that parents did not summon their children home, even during the holidays. Visits by parents were also strongly discouraged and only allowed at Easter and on prize-giving days. In other words the boys belonged body and soul to the school for the duration of their studies. It was a monastic school founded by a group called the Oratorians, who encouraged a rationalist approach to education. When Balzac went there it had become very much secularised, with only seven of the sixteen teachers having been members of the original Oratory, and even they had been released from their vows.

Conditions at the school were very Spartan, and the dormitories were generally in a foul unpleasant condition. They were dirty, smelly and infested with various creatures. The washing facilities consisted of buckets of cold water supplied every morning. In general, conditions were more like those of a prison, with each dormitory divided into six-foot-wide cubicles, barred across the top and with iron gratings on the doors. The boys were locked in every night, to prevent them from indulging in whatever kinds of vices the fathers imagined. Also for special punishments the boys were either locked in these cell-like cubicles or put in a small dark cupboard which became known as the 'alcove'. It seems likely that Balzac spent on average four days a week in this 'alcove', mainly as punishment for his reluctance to do any of the work required of him. Perversely, the experience of this incarceration inspired Balzac's creative imagination: in the novel *Louis Lambert* the main character, in similar conditions, escapes from the reality of his situation by summoning up memories and bringing them alive to himself.

At the Collège de Vendôme, Balzac was, however, also able to pursue his reading interests. Before arriving at the school he had already familiarised himself with the *Iliad* and *Robinson Crusoe*, and now, while taking extra lessons on mathematics in the school library, he was able to explore other kinds of literature. Stories of early Christian martyrs particularly took his fancy. The first real signs of his skill with language are evidenced by his winning of prizes for Latin prose. And he developed several friendships which proved to be influential: with Louis-Lambert Tinant, whose name he most likely borrowed for the novel based on his experiences at the school; and with Barchou de Penhoën, who later became a professor of philosophy, and who undoubtedly stimulated Balzac's interest in metaphysics.

One teacher, Lazare-François Mareschal, was very popular among the pupils. He was also something of a dabbler in literary production, indulging himself in erotic verse and political eulogies. Mareschal's brother-in-law, Jean-Philibert Dessaignes, was also a teacher at the school, and greatly respected for his knowledge and experiments in science. He had even been recognised by the Académie des Sciences for his experiments in magnetism and phosphorescence. It is highly likely that Balzac's interest in explaining intangible forces, such as thought, in terms of rational and material processes, derived from some of the ideas of Dessaignes. It is known that Balzac drafted a 'treatise on will power' in this period, in which there is evidence of this mode of thinking. But he was also developing more literary interests and even attempted an epic poem on the destruction of the Empire of the Incas by Spain.

A mysterious illness finally caused Balzac to leave the school. His parents were summoned to fetch him. In the absence of more precise clinical data, it is impossible to give an exact diagnosis at this distance in time, but Balzac's condition has all the appearances of complete mental and physical fatigue. His sister Laure has related the interpretation which Balzac himself provided of his condition. He felt he was suffering from too much intellectual activity probably caused by an excessive amount of reading in the school library.[2] It is also likely, however, that his frequent enforced stays in his cell and the 'alcove', finally took their toll on him.

Balzac's parents allowed Honoré only about two months to recover and then packed him off to the Lycée Charlemagne in the Marais district of Paris. He stayed in the Ganser-Beuzelin boarding-school, which served also as an annexe to the nearby lycée. The Marais was to feed him with much material for his later writings. It had once been an aristocratic quarter, but by the end of the seventeenth century many tradesmen were living in the area, and when Balzac arrived there it had already become a little seedy, with an odd mixture of social types, including the police spies who would later feature in his novel, *Splendeurs et Misères des Courtisanes* (*A Harlot High and Low*, 1847).

Balzac stayed in Paris for only eight months, and the evidence for his various pursuits during this time is very fragmentary. It is clear, however, that he visited various districts of the city and savoured their atmosphere, even if he could not indulge himself in the delights they had to offer at that time (such as certain theatres, restaurants and the dubious haunts of the Palais-Royal, which was frequented by prostitutes). By now, Napoleon's glory was fading, and it was likely that the monarchy would soon be restored. Balzac's mother became ever more concerned for her son, who had been brought up to admire the emperor. She arranged to have him brought back to Tours, but while in Paris became involved in an affair with a certain Spanish nobleman by the name of Ferdinand de Hérédia, Comte de Prado Castellane. Balzac was to parody the affair in his novel *Le Lys dans la Vallée* (1836).

On the way back to Tours, Balzac contemplated suicide, but was thwarted by the high walls along the bridge over the Loire, into which he proposed to throw himself. It is not clear to what extent Balzac's suicidal intentions were prompted by learning of his mother's affair, or whether he simply felt neglected by her.

By the age of fifteen, Honoré was now feeling strongly the stirrings of desire, though one would not think it from his sister Laure's account of his life. Various young women are mentioned in his fictional accounts of the period, but it is difficult to identify any of them with any certainty. Much of his passion was sublimated in his adoration of the Loire valley's natural beauty.

From July to September 1814, Balzac attended the Collège de Tours as a day boy and was awarded two prizes for his achievements there. As a result, he was also decorated with the Order of the Lily, for evidence in his studies of devotion to King Louis XVIII. It is likely that the award was as much for his father's publication of pamphlets expressing his patriotic fervour as for the son's scholarly achievements.

In the winter of 1814, the family moved back to Paris, taking a house in the Rue du Temple on the western side of the Marais district. At the beginning of 1815, Honoré became a pupil at Lepître school, where he was a boarder, even though the school

was only a few streets from his home. The school sent its board-
ers to the Collège Charlemagne, under an arrangement similar
to that of the Ganser-Beuzelin school. While at the school
Balzac became involved in some protests of pro-Napoleonic
sympathy organised by the wife of the director, Mme Lepître,
very much to the dismay of the royalist M. Lepître himself.
It seems likely that Balzac's admiration was more for the image
of ideal leadership that Bonaparte symbolised than for the politics he represented.

The concierge of the school aided the pupils in their indul-
gence in certain vices, by helping them to smuggle in such things
as forbidden books and the means of making that beverage
to which Balzac was to become addicted and which will always
be closely associated with him: coffee. As a result he ran up considerable debts, and it was his mother who had to bail him out.

He left the Lepître boarding school and returned to that of
Ganser-Beuzelin for the final part of his early education. There
should be no illusions that Balzac had become an accomplished
linguist during his period of attendance at these two schools. On
leaving the latter establishment his mother wrote to him lament-
ing his abysmal performance in Latin: he had come 32nd in
the Latin unseen examination. His mother now decided that it
was her duty to fill in the lamentable gaps in her son's education,
especially with regard to his lack of knowledge about science.
It is likely that these studies focused especially on phrenology
and the theories on magnetism developed by Mesmer, as she
herself was acquainted with both these fields. (There is also
evidence of Balzac's knowledge of them in the novels.) At the
same time, he obtained his first employment as a junior clerk in
the chambers of his father's lawyer friend, Guillonet-Merville.
He also enrolled as a student of law at the École de Droit, situated in the Latin quarter of the city. His experience as a junior
clerk was to provide invaluable material and atmospheric detail, which he would mine in future works. He worked in a large,
smelly, dusty and overheated room. Here he learned of the

miserable fates of people who had fallen foul of the law: the painful disputes between family members over inheritance, spouses stealing from each other, and conspiracies to murder. While he was experiencing the everyday realities in the clerks' office, he learned about the legal concepts and definitions pertaining to them through the lectures at the École de Droit.

In the same period of 1816 to 1818, however, he also at various times attended courses at the Sorbonne. The courses of some of the younger professors were particularly popular at the time. Abel-François Villemain (1790–1870) was teaching literature in a refreshingly new way. He made students aware of the historical and social context of works of literature as well as encouraging their individual sensitivity to them. He also made them familiar with literary works from other cultures, including Shakespeare, Byron and Goethe. Particularly influential was the philosopher Victor Cousin, who encouraged students to reach their own conclusions and not necessarily to accept his own. He is known for introducing the ideas of the German philosopher Immanuel Kant to France. Balzac also attended lectures by Georges Cuvier (1769–1832) at the Museum of Natural History, and was greatly stimulated by his theories on early civilisations, based on available archaeological evidence. Something of Balzac's enthusiasm at this time is captured in the review of western culture and knowledge in the early part of *La Peau de Chagrin* (1831).

In April 1818, Balzac entered the chambers of Victor Passez, the family solicitor. These chambers were located in the very building in which the family was living. Here Balzac was able to learn the ins and outs of selling property and bankruptcy, and how to draw up relevant contracts. Balzac was not the only aspiring writer to have experienced the complexities of the legal world through these chambers. The budding young playwright, Eugène Scribe, had worked there a short time before, and a certain Jules Janin, to become famous in the future as a critic, was at one time the messenger boy. Thanks to the writing of one of the clerks in the office, we also know something about Balzac's appearance at the time: he was actually quite slim (not yet the rather rotund figure of the later portraits) and had a rather florid complexion.[3]

In 1818, Balzac also decided that his fate was probably to become a philosopher, and he began work on a treatise which he entitled 'Discourse on the Immortality of the Soul'. From the material extant relating to this proposed work it is possible to gain considerable insight into Balzac's preoccupations and convictions at the time. He condemned the notion of immortality as being a superstitious fantasy. There is also an unfinished essay from this period on the nature of poetic genius, and there are indications of Balzac's insatiable pursuit of universality in knowledge. He attempted to make a list of the entire range of human intellectual pursuits, amounting to 164 items, and including not only mainstream fields of research such as medicine and the various branches of natural science but also obscure and dubious fields, such as necromancy and demonography. His attempt later in life to incorporate all his literary work within a grandiose scheme of 'human comedy' is not therefore without precedent in his mode of thought. In the extant writings of this period, Balzac can be perceived as trying to reconcile mystical modes of thought with those of current scientific methodology.

Another influential figure in Balzac's life at this time was outside the worlds of both law and academia. Balzac frequently spent holidays with a seventy-year-old friend of his father, Louis-Philippe de Villers-La-Faye (1749–1822), who was mayor of L'Isle-Adam, situated north-west of Paris on the Oise river. Villers-La-Faye had formerly been a priest and was greatly influenced by Voltaire. The two men enjoyed each other's company greatly and Villers-La-Faye encouraged Balzac in the pursuit of three sources of pleasure: boar-hunting, dancing and the company of attractive local girls.

In 1819, a sequence of events occurred which were to change Balzac's life dramatically, and catapult him into determined and focused attempts to establish himself as a man of letters.

His father was due for retirement in April of that year, but due primarily to bureaucratic inefficiency, he could not obtain a full pension. Also, he had invested a considerable amount of money in his employer's bank which had been declared insolvent in 1817. In order to economise, the family had to move to the small town of Villeparisis, north-east of Paris. In the same year occurred the strange case concerning an uncle of Honoré's on his father's side. Louis Balssa was found guilty of strangling a peasant woman who was six months pregnant and he was executed on 16th August. It seems likely from evidence adduced later, that he was actually innocent, but the whole incident upset the family considerably at the time and may have been one of the reasons for moving house and starting afresh. Then, after Balzac passed his first law baccalauréat at the start of 1819, the École de Droit was closed at the beginning of July. Due to a public controversy over property rights among returning émigré royalists, confrontations occurred between members of the school and government troops and it was eventually closed down. Balzac took the opportunity to give up his position with Victor Passez, even though the latter had made him the offer of a fulltime job. He proclaimed to his parents that he wanted to become a writer.

In the face of Honoré's resolute determination, his parents – remarkably, given their perilous financial state – acceded to his wishes. Perhaps they were thinking that a taste of the realities of a writer's existence would finally knock some sense into him. They gave him two years to prove himself and in August he was found a plain little room at the eastern edge of the Marais district, near the Bibliothèque de l'Arsenal. They would keep up the pretence in the meantime that he had gone to live with relatives in the town of Albi.

Thus began the period in Balzac's life which has become idealised and mythologised in the popular imagination through the image of the writer as a poor recluse living in a garret and stimulating his creativity through endless cups of coffee.

Apprentice, Plagiarist and Printer
1819 – 28

The myths that have grown up around the period when Balzac stayed in 9, Rue Lesdiguières, during 1819 and 1820, have their foundation not in fact but in Balzac's own fertile imagination. For him it was a garret with dirty yellow walls. In the introduction to his *Études Philosophiques* (1834) he referred to himself as 'taking refuge in an attic'. In fact it was neither garret nor attic but a decent room on the third floor of the building. Nor did he live on a sparse diet of bread, nuts, water and the like, without contact with other human beings. The old family housekeeper came frequently to bring letters to and fro, dealt with all his laundry and supplied him with fresh vegetables. A family friend, Théodore Dablin, knew of the arrangement and the need for secrecy, and would visit him occasionally. Members of his family also called by to see him from time to time.

Balzac indulged his fertile imagination not only in romanticising his abode but also in working on various philosophical and literary projects. With access to the nearby Bibliothèque de l'Arsenal, he made a translation of Spinoza's *Ethics*. Other essays reveal a preoccupation with Descartes. Then, putting aside his philosophical interests, he planned an opera called *Le Corsaire*, based on a work of Byron about a pirate called Conrad. In the absence of a willing composer, however, the project came to nothing.

With his next project he had more success: a five-act tragedy in rhyming alexandrine couplets on the topic of *Cromwell*. To give himself a clear goal he actually calculated its precise proportions: it should have 2,000 lines and between 8 and 10,000 thoughts.[4] It was a popular subject for treatment in the period, and one of Balzac's own teachers, Abel-François Villemain, had just published a study of the man entitled *Histoire de Cromwell*. Many contemporary French people could also readily identify Cromwell with Napoleon. The play reveals clear sympathies on Balzac's part for the monarchy. It is nowadays rather a laborious read, and the author obviously felt very restricted by the classic metrical form. It was finished in the spring of 1820, coming out at a little shorter than his prescription: 1,906 lines. Balzac went to his family home in Villeparisis and read it before his assembled family, who clearly found it very boring. Balzac himself eventually came to see that his play lacked any real merit.

Balzac now attempted to comfort himself by plunging into a bout of novel-reading. Contemporary French novels consisted mainly of rambling plots with moral points at the end and the most popular works imported from abroad were in the Gothic vein, including those of Ann Radcliffe, Matthew 'Monk' Lewis and so on. The first writer popular at the time to fire Balzac's imagination was undoubtedly Sir Walter Scott. He admired Scott's capacity to evoke mood and nature and reflect character in quite realistic dialogue. Scott's exoticism, and sense of history and adventure, enlivened by convincing descriptive detail, also greatly impressed him. Balzac's own first attempts at writing novels date from this period.

The earliest of these attempts at novel-writing, none of which were ever completed, was probably *Sténie*, which was started near the end of 1819 and given up probably in 1822. It had the subtitle *Les Erreurs Philosophiques* (*Philosophical Errors*) and was written as a sequence of letters. The story is about the love of a young man, Job, for the young woman who was raised by the same nurse and who is therefore like a sister to him. After being separated they meet again during their adolescence and fall in love, but the girl, Sténie, is already engaged to another man. There are many autobiographical elements in the novel and it would seem to be no coincidence that Balzac started work on it at a time when his own sister Laure was going out with the man who became her own future husband.

After Laure was married in 1820, Balzac started work on another novel, *Falthurne*, which is more notable for its use of fantastic elements. The story is set vaguely in tenth-century Naples at the time of the Norman invasion of Italy and deals with the opposition of the church to the mysterious powers of a certain Falthurne. Balzac used the literary conceit of pretending that the text was a manuscript written by a priest, Abbé Savonati, and discovered by a soldier in Napoleon's army. A school teacher, M. Matricante, translates the text and adds comments of his own on the events depicted. The mysterious Falthurne, it would seem, was reputed to have supernatural powers which enabled him to see into the future and walk through walls.

The next novel Balzac attempted was entitled *Corsino*. Only fifteen pages of it are extant and there is little indication of how the plot might have developed. Corsino is an idealist attempting to combine the simplicity of a life close to nature with the advantages of civilisation. He chooses to live a life of complete self-indulgence in the north of Scotland. Two other characters appear: Maria, an ideally beautiful peasant girl and a friend, whose name, Néhoro, is a clear anagram of Honoré.

During the period when he was working on these novels in the Rue Lesdiguières, Balzac used to indulge himself frequently in wandering around the district dressed in shabby clothes, to observe the local working people and their habits. He felt it enabled him to identify with the local people and enter into their characters. It should be remembered that wandering in the poorer districts of Paris at that time was both a risky and a dirty activity. Very few people wandered such streets unless they really had to. Many of his walks went far beyond his own district, to the factory areas and also to a place which had become fashionable for walks: the Père Lachaise cemetery, which was to feature as a setting for the final part of *Le Père Goriot* (1835).

The lease for Balzac's room expired in 1820, and he went back to Villeparisis, where he would stay intermittently for the next two years. It was a small insignificant township of no more than 500 people, and the Balzacs lived in a plain country-style house backing onto some fields and woodland along the Canal d'Ourcq. Although Balzac was not exactly happy at having to return to the family home, he nevertheless used the opportunity to study family and local life in detail. Aspects of the Balzac family household thus found their way into a novel called *Wann-Chlore*, which was begun in 1822, but not published until 1824. The family enjoyed reading the novel and failed to recognise the portraits of themselves.

It was during this period that Balzac's younger sister, Laurence, entered a disastrous marriage. The family were keen to get her married off, as she was not exactly an attractive match, and when a good-looking man of thirty-three with the imposing name of Amand-Désiré Michaut de Saint-Pierre de Montzaigle showed interest in her, her parents had little hesitation. Although Montzaigle had a reputation for gambling and womanising in his youth, the Balzacs interpreted this favourably as a sign that he was now ready to settle down. In letters to his elder sister Honoré revealed his own serious doubts about the man's character, but made no effective protests. Within months of the marriage, Laurence found herself spending her evenings alone, while her husband spent much of his time and money in casinos. Laurence had to send letters to her parents begging for money. Her general state of mind obviously had a detrimental effect on the state of her health. It was probably not a direct cause of her death at the age of twenty-three in 1825, but may well have contributed to her rapid decline in health after giving birth to her second child. She died destitute.

Laurence had in fact developed strong feelings, shortly after her engagement to Montzaigle, for another man, a young writer friend of Honoré, called Auguste Le Poitevin de l'Égreville, often known more simply as Auguste Lepoitevin. This man was to influence Balzac's literary output directly over the next five years. They entered into an agreement whereby Balzac was to dash off some stories which Lepoitevin would then polish up and sell to publishers. By this agreement Balzac wrote three novels in collaboration with Lepoitevin and six completely on his own. Five of these novels appeared in the one year of 1822 alone.

The dubious but influential figure of Auguste Lepoitevin deserves some attention in his own right. Having perceived that there was a growing demand for popular novels, Lepoitevin was determined to take full advantage of this opportunity. He also became renowned for his gossipy journalism, which he utilised to blackmail prominent people, and nowadays is remembered mainly for being the editor in the 1840s of a scandal sheet called *Le Corsaire-Satan*. At one time even the poet Charles Baudelaire wrote for him. Lepoitevin may not have discovered Balzac exactly but he certainly helped set him on his way.

Balzac's family, however, started to become concerned that these popular novels might bring their name into disrepute and they insisted that Honoré adopt a pseudonym. With his liking for anagrams Balzac settled for 'Lord R'Hoone'. Lepoitevin, incidentally, published under the name Viellerglé (an anagram of 'L'Égreville').

One of these novels was *L'Héritière de Birague*, completed in 1821. It was yet another work supposedly discovered as a manuscript written by a monk and published by Lepoitevin and Balzac. It tells of a dastardly selfish man who blackmails the mother of a beautiful young girl in order to possess her daughter. The two men were not above writing their own reviews of their works and publishing them also under other pseudonyms. One of the novels written by Balzac on his own was a light frolic called *Jean-Louis ou La Fille Trouvée*, about a handsome working-class lad who remains faithful to his girlfriend despite the attempts of other women to seduce him. In *Le Vicaire des Ardennes* (1822), he used again the device of pretending that the story was a discovered manuscript, this time taken from a dying man. This work marked the end of his partnership with Lepoitevin: for Balzac had already found himself a new publisher. It was at about this time too that he became involved in his first real love affair, with the wife of a neighbour in Villeparisis, Mme Laure de Berny.

Balzac first got to know Mme de Berny as tutor to her children. He enjoyed the aristocratic air of her house in contrast to his own. And she had significant connections: her father, a German named Joseph Hinner, was harpist to the Queen, and her mother had been a chambermaid to Marie Antoinette. Her godparents were no less than the King and Queen themselves. She was forty-five years old and an intelligent and passionate woman. Unfortunately, few of Balzac's letters in the next four years have survived, and those to Mme de Berny were burned at her request after she died in 1836. The rough drafts of those for the year 1822, however, have survived. They reveal a man preoccupied with wooing and seducing her with all the literary skills at his command. She resisted, stressing the fact that she was a wife and mother and too old for him. Finally she softened, and in May 1822, she agreed to a night-time rendezvous in her garden, where they sat on a bench and exchanged their first kiss. The relationship inspired his writing directly: at her instigation he started to make notes about conducting an adulterous relationship, which were to be transformed eventually into an essay a few years later on how to avoid it, *La Physiologie du Mariage* (1829). Balzac's mother eventually got to know of this relationship and tried to prevent its further development by sending her son off to Bayeux. But this did not dampen his ardour. In November of that year the Balzac family moved back to the Marais district of Paris again for a time, and even then the lovers managed to arrange meetings in the city.

In Paris Balzac had a lucky encounter with a publisher called Charles Alexandre Pollet (1776–1834), whose company, the *Librairie Théâtral et Romantique*, was becoming very successful, especially through its publication of currently popular plays. Balzac signed a contract for his next two novels, *Le Centenaire* and *Le Vicaire des Ardennes*, to appear under the pseudonym 'Horace de Saint-Aubin'. In the first of these, published in November 1822, the centenarian of the title believes that if he can acquire nubile young girls regularly for his pleasure he will live for ever, and eventually become omniscient. The book caused a sensation among many of the critics.

The second novel, *Le Vicaire des Ardennes*, appearing close on the heels of the first one, was also a success. It was written in an unusual way: Balzac's sister Laure and her husband provided the plot and some of the chapters, which Balzac himself then re-wrote, as well as contributing some chapters himself. There were many delays and for a time it seemed as if Balzac would not meet his deadline. Eventually he found himself in a situation which was to become all too common in his career: while some parts of the novel were already at the printers, he was still writing the rest. The novel has a complex and confusing plot, focusing on a new curate and a mysterious pirate, but the characterisation of the village folk is lively and one of the work's most accomplished aspects. It is this novel which was the first to show the influence of the ideas of Johann Kaspar Lavater (1741–1801), whose work entitled *The Art of Knowing Men by Their Physiognomy* had already been so influential in German literary circles. The theme of incest accidentally indulged in gained for it condemnation by the church, and on 26th November 1822, the novel was banned, the manuscript removed from the Balzac home, and all available copies confiscated. After a thorough investigation, however, the matter was dropped, mainly due to the inefficient bureaucracy handling the affair. Balzac lost no time in following up with a sequel to *Le Vicaire des Ardennes* entitled *Annette et le Criminel*.

After this, Balzac began to devote more of his time to journalism for a while. In this he was helped by a man who acted as a kind of literary agent for him, long before such figures became commonplace. This was Horace-Napoleon Raisson (1798–1854). Among the works that they produced together were many handbooks of practical social advice, on such matters as being honest, talking about and selling literature, etc. Balzac still had no qualms about writing favourable reviews of his own works and also occasionally writing as devil's advocate for causes that he did not believe in. One such example was an issue hotly debated at the time: the right of inheritance by the eldest son, or primogeniture (*droit d'aînesse*). Balzac was against it at the time but wrote an article in its defence. Ironically, he later came to recognise the usefulness of the law as a bastion against social chaos. Shortly after this he also published anonymously a history of the Jesuits (*Histoire Impartiale des Jésuites*), in which he strove to be objective, suppressing his own more liberal views.

One friend of Balzac's at that time who was to become influential in directing him towards a more conservative way of thinking, and especially towards Catholicism, was Jean Thomassy, who had studied law in Paris: though Balzac probably met him through a publisher. It was under Thomassy's influence, for example, that Balzac started to write a treatise on prayer.

At the end of 1823, Balzac submitted a melodrama, *Le Nègre*, to the Gaîté Theatre. It was rejected as being badly constructed and basically immoral. It dealt with the risqué subject of the love of a black servant for his master's wife. Under his pseudonym of Horace de Saint-Aubin, Balzac also published a reworking of the Aladdin story entitled *La Dernière Fée ou La Nouvelle Lampe Merveilleuse*. It tells of a young man who has grown up close to nature and believing in fairies. One day, he meets the fairy of his dreams, who actually turns out to be an English duchess.

In 1824, Balzac moved into an apartment of a house on the corner of the Rue Saint-Sulpice and the Rue de Tournon. His recent novels had not received very favourable reviews. He still maintained his partnership with Raisson, producing various dubious semi-plagiarised texts. In the latter part of 1825, his novel *Wann-Chlore* was published but with no mention of the author's name and it aroused little interest in the press. In the same year, Balzac worked on a grandiose plan of an extensive social history of France, which he would entitle *Histoire de France Pittoresque* and in which he aimed not to recount the political events, but to capture the spirit of each age.

While seeking a publisher for *Wann-Chlore*, Balzac met the publisher Urbain Canel, who inspired him with the idea for an original publishing venture. The plan was to produce the complete works of classic French authors in one portable volume for each author and at a reasonable price. Balzac gained the support of a family friend who had money to invest and also of Mme de Berny. The first two volumes were to be on Molière and La Fontaine. But the whole venture rapidly became a disaster. Booksellers were not willing to risk stocking the books, the print-size of the words was too small, and despite original intentions, the price was too high. Though they ran up an enormous deficit on the project, Balzac felt that he had learned much from their failure. Money, he decided, was in the process of printing itself. With the support of Mme de Berny and her husband, he bought a printing works which had just come on the market in the Rue des Marais-Saint-Germain. He employed about thirty workers and ran up a debt of about 70,000 francs. He was to live in the very building which housed the printing works for the next two years.

In 1826, there was a family scandal to deal with. Balzac's father took advantage of his wife's absence from Villeparisis (she was away in Touraine) to make a local girl pregnant. He was seventy-nine years old at the time. When his mother found out she managed to have the whole affair covered up, but the family decided to leave Villeparisis for Versailles, to put the shameful incident well and truly behind them.

At about this time, Balzac got to know the mother of an old friend of his sister Laure. She was the Duchesse d'Abrantès, and to add to the confusion her name, too, was Laure. (It was perhaps for this reason that Balzac preferred to call her Marie.) The young Honoré was attracted not only by her physical charms but by her connections: she had been married to one of Napoleon's most distinguished generals, Andoche Junot, Duc d'Abrantès. The Duchess hinted that she had even been Napoleon's lover at one time. Balzac agreed to help her write her memoirs. For some time he divided his affections between the Duchess and Mme de Berny, who now visited him almost every day, trying to persuade him that the Duchess was manipulating him.

The first works produced by Balzac's printing works were not exactly impressive. There was a leaflet advertising the products of a local pharmacist, and booklets providing advice on subjects such as how to settle debts or how to avoid dining at home. Balzac also printed political texts of all possible persuasions. All comers were welcome. If nothing else, the business brought him into contact with some of the leading literary figures of the day, including Victor Hugo and Alfred de Vigny. Balzac may have spent his days as a printer besmirched with ink, but he now spent many an evening in the rarefied air of literary salons, such as that of the famous Mme Récamier. But in order to be accepted in such circles, Balzac found he had to spend much of his hard-earned income from printing on clothes. And the printing works was not exactly thriving. Debts were mounting and Balzac and his partner Barbier were forced to sell off both machinery and premises and rent them back at a yearly rate. These measures were not to prove effective, and Balzac sank ever more deeply into debt. Outwardly, however, he maintained the impression of solvency, even purchasing a type-foundry in September 1827. It is in fact typical of Balzac's psychology that he wanted to gain control of the whole process of printing and publishing books. But in April 1828, the entire business enterprise collapsed. Balzac now found himself owing 50,000 francs to his mother and a similar amount to Mme de Berny, who took over the company and put it in the hands of her own son, Alexandre. Within a short time, under Alexandre's management, it became one of the most successful printing companies in Paris.

Balzac's business sense can be described as imaginative but reckless. He would willingly accept dubious promissory notes in lieu of payment and give impossibly generous discounts. He had many ideas which were ahead of his time but he failed to realise them efficiently. For example, he developed a plan for an organisation which would have been the forerunner of a modern book-club; he also dreamed of producing an encyclopaedia especially for children. To be fair to him, the economic climate was not exactly favourable to his experiments. A recession had started in 1826, which lasted well into 1830, by which time about 2,500 people a year were being declared bankrupt in Paris alone. Balzac's reaction to his situation was not to rein in his expenditure but to continue it in a different direction. He indulged himself in ever more stylish clothes and rented a charming little villa on the outskirts of the city under the name of M. Surville (his sister Laure's married name) with the help of his friend Hyacinthe de Latouche. He planned to devote himself to writing a historical novel. It was at this time that he decided to publish under the name 'Honoré Balzac'.

Recognition and Critical Success
1828–32

Balzac had become interested in the history of the uprisings which took place in the western part of France between 1793 and 1800, when supporters of the Royalists had opposed the new Republic. In the autumn of 1828, he set off for Fougères in Brittany, to stay in the home of Gilbert de Pommereul, the son of one of Balzac's father's friends. General Pommereul had fought for Napoleon in a campaign against the guerrilla fighters, who were known as the 'Chouans', probably after a dialect word for the cry of an owl, which they used to give signals to each other. Balzac realised that many participants in the events were still alive, and would be able to give firsthand accounts of the atrocities committed: families had been divided by their political loyalties and murderous raids had been carried out on neighbouring communities. It should not be assumed, however, that the resulting novel, *Les Chouans*, published in 1828, was closely based on facts. Balzac changed many details, including sequences of events, the characters involved and the local geography. While taking notes on the actual locations of events, he also summoned up the scenes with his own imagination.

Balzac stayed with the general's family for about six weeks, during which time he also gathered material based on families known to the Pommereuls, material which he would use later in a collection of tales called *Scènes de la Vie Privée* (the first of which were published in 1830). On returning to Paris, Balzac got down to finishing *Les Chouans*, which took him about four to five weeks. It was published in 1829 under his own name 'M. Honoré Balzac'. The critical reception, however, was not very positive. It seems that readers were not happy with the combination of a love story and complex historical events. Many modern readers also find that the work is very long and complicated. However, it has subsequently come to be considered a perceptive historical study, which reveals an understanding of the trends of the period.

It is clear that the presence of Balzac's friend, Hyacinthe de Latouche, aided and influenced the production of *Les Chouans*. There has been much speculation about the nature of Balzac's relationship with Latouche: to what extent did it have a homosexual basis? Latouche was reticent about his own undoubted talent as a writer but encouraged that of others, including Balzac. When Balzac moved to his new villa, Latouche helped him choose and fit the wallpaper. When George Sand visited Balzac's house a few years later, she found it very feminine in character, like a collection of ladies' boudoirs.[5] Many of Balzac's letters of the period were destroyed in a fire, and those that remain reveal only the bickering and critical attitude each of the friends took towards the other's works. But they had planned and indeed tried to live together, and so some strength of mutual feeling must have persisted for some time.

It is also undeniable that several of Balzac's descriptions of relationships between men in his novels hint at sexual attraction. In particular, three recurring characters in *La Comédie humaine* are ambiguous in their sexuality: Lucien de Rubempré, Eugène de Rastignac and Vautrin. In *Illusions Perdues* (1836), David Sèchard adores his friend Lucien de Rubempré, taking pleasure in obeying him and observing his beauty. Lucien is also described as enjoying the attention like a woman who knows she is loved. If this echoes Balzac's own life, then Latouche was the adoring one. Latouche's letters frequently reveal his feelings for Honoré, but Balzac, fourteen years junior to Latouche, does not seem to have found the older man attractive. Balzac was also acquainted with other known homosexuals, however, which aroused some suspicions amongst his contemporaries. A few years later, Balzac was to take under his wing several younger men, who give cause for more speculation about his own feelings. Perhaps he was catholic in his tastes. Two of his stories, 'Sarrasine' and 'Une Passion dans le Désert', both published in 1830, shortly after his break up with Latouche, deal with sexual confusion: the love of a sculptor for someone he believes to be a woman but who turns out to be a castrato, and a soldier's feelings for the sensuous body of a panther he finds sleeping next to him.

In June 1829, Balzac's father died in his eighty-second year. The immediate cause had been a coach accident, but his son suspected that the various pills his father had been taking had had serious side effects. Balzac was away from home at the time, and it seems unlikely that he was able to return in time for the funeral. He inherited all his father's money, but as this had to be handed over immediately to his mother, his financial situation was in no way improved. Several of the stories written and published in the period immediately after his father's death, reveal a preoccupation with death and mourning. One story in particular, depicting rather horrible events, is worthy of note. It is 'El Verdugo', in which a son (of the same age as Balzac) has to defend the family's honour by chopping off his old father's head.

'El Verdugo' was also the first work to be signed with the particle 'de', as 'Honoré de Balzac'. It seems that Balzac wanted to attain some level of success before making his aristocratic pretensions public. There had been a medieval family called the Balzacs d'Entragues, and it was to this branch that Balzac claimed a connection, though the line had long died out. Whatever his justification, the 'de' enabled him to gain easier access to the higher levels of society.

Although unable to afford even some basic necessities for himself at this time, Balzac nevertheless paid for the services of a maid, called Flore. In the latter part of 1829 he shut himself away in his house for days on end, working variously on *La Physiologie du Mariage*, which he had made a printed version of in 1826 but never published, and *Scènes de la Vie Privée*.

Early in 1830, as well as writing stories, Balzac planned to take up playwriting again. One such plan was for a play version of the Don Juan legend in collaboration with Eugène Sue. But none of Balzac's dramatic plans were realised. The work which established him as a known literary figure, and which finally appeared at this time, was *La Physiologie du Mariage*. For a long time Balzac was referred to, in conversation and by critics, as the author of this work. His critique of the institution of marriage was generally felt to be timely, and one reviewer even recommended that newlyweds study it after their honeymoon. It was also clear that Balzac had tapped a vast audience which was poorly catered for at the time: that of women.

To improve his financial circumstances, Balzac started writing for several newspapers. Furthering his journalistic interests, he had befriended another journalist, Émile de Girardin. Together with Balzac, Hippolyte Auger, and some other writers, Girardin founded the *Feuilleton des Journaux Politiques*, which mainly contained reviews of the latest books. Girardin also founded another journal, aptly named *Le Voleur* (*The Thief*), for it stole most of its articles from other magazines. While this periodical was in many ways irresponsible, it had the serious intention of criticising the values of the bourgeoisie. Balzac's most satirical comments were included in another publication, also founded by Girardin, called *La Mode*. This was the first magazine in France to write seriously for women, treating them as intelligent, critical readers. In his comments on fashion, Balzac stressed how dress revealed cultural and social trends. Clothes were an index of social class. This was well ahead of its time and prefigures some aspects of the ideas of the twentieth-century writer Roland Barthes. Balzac's journalism in this period, from the end of 1829 to the middle of 1831, did manage to fulfil his most pressing need: it provided an adequate income.

The year 1830 saw significant political changes in France. The restoration of the monarchy had led also to the reaffirmation of the privileges of the nobility and the church. King Charles X ignored the electoral defeat in June and July of that year and clamped down on free speech, also dissolving the newly elected chamber. After three days of riots in the streets, the king fled to England and Louis-Philippe was put on the throne as a constitutional monarch. During this period of momentous events Balzac was actually out of Paris in Touraine staying in a charming house called La Grenadière on the banks of the Loire overlooking Tours. Mme de Berny stayed with Balzac for part of this time, although their love was now cooling into friendship. In June they made a trip down the Loire to Nantes, and visited two places at the furthest point of the estuary: Guérande and Le Croisic. Shortly after this, Mme de Berny returned home, writing to Balzac with the news that she had burnt his letters. Balzac had in any case been growing weary of the clinging nature of her affections. Early in September he went back to Paris by coach.

Back in Paris, he plunged himself into work, sleeping at times for only two hours a night. It is from this period that he started to wear a monk's habit and to indulge himself more excessively in endless cups of coffee. He also began to involve himself more directly in politics. He attempted to persuade the people around Fougères, under General Pommereul's influence, to support him in the forthcoming election. Balzac, however, had overlooked one crucial detail: as he was not a landowner, and paid no taxes, he was not actually eligible to stand for parliament. The election came and went, but Balzac was not deterred and hoped to try his luck in a by-election in Chinon in 1832.

At the same time, he planned a philosophical novel, *La Peau de Chagrin*, which appeared in 1831 and proved to be one of his masterpieces. It tells the story of a young man, Raphaël de Valentin, who is tired of his life but defers throwing himself into the Seine by browsing in an old curiosity shop. After wandering through a hoard of mysterious objects which embody the whole of western culture and beyond, he is shown an old ass's skin inscribed in Sanskrit. The text promises Valentin the fulfilment of all his wishes, but with each wish the skin will shrivel a little more as his own life will become shorter. Valentin thereby attains his desire of becoming fantastically wealthy, but his health suffers, and as he dies he realises that absolute power is worthless if one does not know how to make use of it. The old shopkeeper had expressed the central insight of the work, that real satisfaction and contentment is to be found not in the heart or the senses but in the mind:

> The exercise of the *will* consumes us; the exercise of *power* destroys us; but the pursuit of *knowledge* leaves our infirm constitution in a state of perpetual calm.[6]

Many have seen the work also as an allegory of post-revolutionary France, in which the priorities of civilisation appeared to be mainly materialistic. The book went on sale on 1st August 1831, barely two days after Balzac had finished writing it. Due to extensive publicity it was sold out immediately. There were a few critical responses but most people recognised its unique qualities immediately, and it was so popular with the general public that a second edition was brought out in September, together with twelve other stories, under the title *Romans et Contes Philosophiques*. The esteem with which the book was regarded inevitably led to parodies, both on the stage, at the Gaîté Theatre, and in print, by the young poet Théophile Gautier.

In August 1831, Balzac published another small masterpiece, which should not be overlooked, 'Le Chef-d'oeuvre Inconnu' ('The Unknown Masterpiece'). A great artist, called Frenhofer, has been working on the same painting for ten years. He considers it so beautiful that he worships it as though it were his mistress. One of the man's pupils and the famous artist Nicolas

Poussin are vouchsafed a viewing of it, but what they see is different to that vision in the artist's mind: 'All I see are colours daubed one on top of the other and contained by a mass of strange lines forming a wall of paint.'[7] Apparently both Cézanne and Picasso admired the story and identified with the artist in it. Picasso even produced an illustrated edition of the story.

During this time, the writer Eugène Sue, who became famous for long serial novels reflecting social ills, had an especially strong influence on Balzac's life. Through him Balzac gained a wider perspective on the social world. In particular, Sue granted him access to a special area in the Opéra known as the 'Infernal Box', where fashionable young men would gather to comment loudly on the singers during the actual performance. Sue also introduced his friend to the delights of smoking cigars.

Success tempted Balzac into an orgy of spending. In September 1831, he rented another part of the house in which he was already living, bought a pair of horses, a carriage, and acquired a shed to house it. Two more servants were employed, as well as a highly qualified cook called Rose.

In the spring of 1832, during a cholera epidemic, the first collection of ten of the *Contes Drolatiques* (usually known in English as the *Droll Tales*), were published. These were part of an ongoing plan throughout Balzac's life, to produce a large collection of stories in the scurrilous style of Rabelais. Balzac intended to produce a hundred of them, but in the event only thirty were published in three sets of ten. The pretence was maintained that the stories were collected from the monasteries of the Touraine area. Some were original inventions by Balzac and others were parodies of already existing tales. They were written in a quirky style: Balzac's own version of Medieval French. Typical of the tone and theme of the stories is 'La Belle Impéria', which recounts a priest's experience of spending the evening with a famous courtesan, Impéria, who specialises in satisfying the needs of highly placed men of the church. Some of the tales verge on the downright tasteless, and are blatantly scatological.

To fulfil the legal requirements as candidate for the by-election in Chinon in 1832, Balzac sought out some property near Vouvray, and to improve his image he also tried to acquire a wife, preferably a rich one. In the event, he did not stand for election, realising that there was little hope of his winning in the face of apathy on the part of the voters. On a trip to stir up interest among the voters in Chinon, he had a bad accident: as he was stepping down from his carriage, he fell and hit his head on the paving stones, and lay there, dazed, for twenty minutes or so. Balzac was forced to stay in bed for several days and was nursed at his sister's house where he was put on a special diet, bled, and told to refrain from intellectual activity. It seems that the injury affected Balzac's ability to coordinate language, and the wrong words occurred to him frequently.

Whether or not it was related to the after-effects of his fall, there was considerable concern for some time amongst family and friends for Balzac's sanity. The verbal confusions that Balzac was experiencing are now thought to have been symptoms of a disorder of the linguistic faculty which had not yet been given a name at the time, but which is now called aphasia. It cannot be said, however, that this was a direct result of the accident, because it recurred throughout Balzac's life in various forms and may signify some congenital defect. Balzac utilised his own linguistic problems in one of his most autobiographical novels: *Louis Lambert* (published in October 1832), which tells of a genius who goes insane. Much of Balzac's own childhood is incorporated into the novel, including his experiences at the Collège de Vendôme. The narrator is described as the best friend of the genius, but the main character and narrator can easily be perceived as two sides of the same personality. There is an interesting report that Balzac met the German scientist and explorer Alexander von Humboldt in the salon of Baron Gérard, and that they discussed the latest psychological theories and the concept of madness.

Success had not solved Balzac's financial problems, however, and the nagging reminders about his debts which his mother sent him while he was in Saché did not help his general state of mind. At this time he was also thinking about a collection of stories, which can be classed as 'detective stories'. They were to be published in 1833 under the title *Histoire des Treize* (*History of the Thirteen*). The thirteen men of the title were a mysterious group deemed to have power and influence in every corner of society, unseen manipulators, with their own selfish, evil ends. In his own preface Balzac lends them an archetypal status:

they were undoubtedly criminals, but undeniably remarkable for certain qualities which go to the making of great men, and they recruited their members only from among men of outstanding quality...
... they were the very incarnations of ideas suggested to the imagination by the fantastic powers attributed to the Manfreds, Fausts and Melmoths of literature.[8]

During the month he spent in Saché in 1832, it became quite clear that Balzac was at times living in a world in which he took his own dreams and plans for reality. He often stated that he had already written novels which had, in fact, not progressed beyond a title and vague outline. His correspondence with his publishers reveals the discrepancies between what he was telling them and what had actually been achieved. Perhaps it was a deliberate ploy to gain their commitment, but friends and relatives were also drawn into the fantasy. In September 1832, Balzac was talking enthusiastically about how he had completed the novel *La Bataille*, but after several weeks of keeping up the illusion he had to admit that he had not written a single word. In 1833, when Louis Mame went to collect the manuscript of the novel *Le Médecin de Campagne* (conceived during the summer of 1832), he found that only chapter summaries existed.

Meanwhile, Balzac's fame was spreading, especially among his female readers. Since *La Femme de Trente Ans*, first published in 1832, in which it had been asserted that a woman only really becomes beautiful in middle age, he had been pestered by unknown beautiful women, many turning up at his door or sending him perfumed letters. Just how hysterical some of them had become is illustrated by a bizarre incident in the summer of 1832. In July, Balzac left Saché and walked to Tours, from where he travelled by coach to Angoulême. The plan was to spend a month with his friends Zulma and François-Michel Carraud, while completing stories he had started recently (he famously completed the story 'La Grenadière' in one day while playing billiards). The young Albéric Second, later a journalist, was staying in the area at the time and recalled in his memoirs that when Balzac went to have his hair cut in the town, the barber's shop was besieged by local women arguing over the possession of locks of his fallen hair.[9]

Zulma's husband was an army officer, fifteen years older than her. Because of his resistance to the new regime he had been posted away from Paris and he seethed with resentment and self-pity. Balzac utilised some aspects of his friends' situation for his story 'Les Marana'. The Spanish woman, Juana, in the story is forced to marry a French army officer to save her honour, but finally stabs him. Balzac was not suggesting the same solution to Zulma, but he did offer to become her lover. He was refused, Zulma preferring to remain good friends. Balzac was, however, already starting another romantic involvement. In 1831 he had received an anonymous letter, the sender of which was later identified as a lady of thirty-six with a most imposing name: Claire-Clémence-Henriette-Claudine de Maillé de La Touer-Landry, Marquise de Castries. She invited Balzac to join her and her uncle, the Duc de Fitz-James, in the spa of Aix-les-Bains. They planned to travel on through Switzerland and down into Italy. Balzac decided to travel directly from Angoulême to Aix-les-Bains, setting off in late August. The Marquise had been ostracised from the salons of the Faubourg Saint-Germain for having an affair with the son of the famous Austrian statesman Metternich. On his arrival in Aix-les-Bains, Balzac found that the

Marquise had arranged everything for his convenience. A reasonably priced room had been reserved for him at the hotel and his meals already paid for. He was free to do as he wished during the daytime but was invited to join the table of the Marquise for dinner. Balzac became determined to seduce the Marquise, despite her age and infirmities. In preparation he ordered new clothes and toiletries to be sent to him from Paris, but all this failed to impress the Marquise. By the time they all arrived in Geneva in early October he had made no progress in his wooing. While in Geneva Balzac attempted to heighten the Romantic atmosphere by taking the Marquise on a drive out to the Villa Diodati, where Mary and Percy Bysshe Shelley had met up with Lord Byron in 1816. It was here that he attempted to make his feelings clear, but he was met with shocked rejection. From the Marquise's point of view it was an affront to her undying love for the young Metternich. Balzac fled back to Paris.

Balzac's anger and disappointment found their expression in some stories while he recovered in the company of Mme de Berny. In 'La Duchesse de Langeais' (1834), a spurned lover threatens to brand his adored duchess with an iron; in one of the *Contes Drolatiques* published during this period, a distraught lover punishes his cruel mistress by slicing off her left cheek.

The Unknown Woman
and the Birth of a Universe
1832–6

One of the most significant events in Balzac's life also occurred in 1832: he received a letter from an unknown woman, posted in Odessa in February of that year. She withheld her name, signing herself simply '*L'Étrangère*'. The original letter has been lost but Balzac's response is extant. Not having an address to write to, he put a small advertisement in the *Gazette de France*, which was also commonly read in Russia. It was discreet and hinted at wishes that could not be expressed in public. This was the start not only of the most dominant emotional relationship of his adult years but also of his most extensive correspondence. The earliest letters date from before the break-up with the Marquise de Castries, revealing the complexity of Balzac's 'womanising'. A second letter came from his mysterious admirer and critic later in the spring. She was critical, expressing some dismay at the author's depiction of women in *La Peau de Chagrin*. In Balzac's early letters to her he poured out his reflections on life, literature and also supplied a potted autobiography. He was moulding her in his own imagination into his muse, the ideal woman who understood him completely and who inspired him to ever greater heights in his writing.

Five or six letters had been exchanged between them by the spring of 1833, and Balzac was imagining her as a young and beautiful woman. He imagined and guessed at all kinds of qualities in her and facts about her life, romanticising her as a Polish princess. On this occasion the reality lived up to the dream: she came from a famous ancient Polish family, the Rzewuskis, who had produced many statesmen and warriors. Her married name was Eveline Hanska, and her father had been a senator of the Empire and lived in a medieval castle at Pohrebyszcze in the Ukraine, where she was born. The exact date of her birth has not been established, but Balzac decided that it was 1806. To help her family out of financial straits she married a rather boring count, Wenceslas Hanski (the masculine form of the family name), twenty years older than her, in 1819. He owned a 21,000 acre estate with thousands of serfs in Wierzchownia, in the region of Kiev. The house was lavishly furnished, with many Renaissance masterpieces, an extensive library and even its own hospital. Its main drawback for a woman of sensitivity was its isolation: there was nothing to distract or entertain a lonely wife. After the loss of four children, the one surviving child, a daughter named Anna, was her only solace. For Eveline Hanska, her correspondence with Balzac was obviously a lifeline. It is also likely that she was jealous of her elder sister, Caroline, who had left her own much older husband and had several affairs, including one with the poet Alexander Pushkin. For Eveline, Balzac also meant contact with the glamorous literary world of Paris.

Unfortunately, only two of Eveline's letters to Balzac have survived. After some of them were stolen from him in 1847, Balzac burned the rest. In the two that survive, Eveline appears to be a well-read and intelligent woman, serious, and with an interest in the occult. In the early stages of their relationship she was determined that they should never meet, but by early 1833 it seems that she did not rule out the possibility. In this year she and her husband visited Vienna, where the count had grown up. He had received a passport only on the condition that he did not visit France for fear of Jacobin influence. In the summer, the couple arrived in Neuchâtel in Switzerland to visit the home of their daughter's governess, Henriette Borel. It seemed that now a meeting with Balzac might be possible.

Balzac left Paris on the evening of 22nd September 1833, and arrived in the town of Besançon on the morning of the 24th. Here he met a young journalist, Charles de Bernard, who was an admirer of his writing and had written favourable reviews of his works in the local press. He attempted to find a certain document in this town which was crucial to the setting up of his plan for a book club. When he could not find it, he set off again impatiently the same evening. He crossed the Jura mountains and went down the next day through the Val de Travers to Neuchâtel. He had travelled for four days without sleeping in a bed.

Eveline Hanska and her husband, with their large entourage of servants, were staying in a big house they had rented called the Maison Andrié. A nearby promenade led to the Crêt, a local promontory with a fine view of the lake. Balzac sent a message to Eveline informing her of his arrival and that he would be waiting for her on the promenade, looking at the lake, between one and four o'clock. As he left his hotel for the assignation he saw a beautiful woman and wondered if it could just possibly be her. Reality was to confirm his romantic daydream: he learned later that it had indeed been her. He also thought he saw her face at the window as he passed the Maison Andrié. When they finally met on the promenade, each was delighted and entranced by the other. Eveline praised, in a letter to her brother, Balzac's lovable and childlike qualities, and in a letter to his sister Laure, Balzac praised her ravishing beauty and also her unspoiled childlike quality, her naivety. Unfortunately Eveline's husband Wenceslas also found Balzac charming and scarcely left the couple alone. Finally, during a trip to an island on the Lac de Bienne, famous for its associations with Jean-Jacques Rousseau, Wenceslas went off to organise the preparation of lunch and the couple were left alone. Under the shade of an oak tree they exchanged their first kiss. They made all kinds of fantastic plans which they hoped would enable them to meet in the future. The one certain thing was that Eveline and her husband planned to spend the winter in Geneva. On 5th October, after going to look at the Maison Andrié for one last time at five o'clock in the morning, while all its inhabitants were asleep, Balzac left Neuchâtel. Arriving at Besançon he spent the day with Charles de Bernard and the local librarian.

Since the start of his correspondence with Eveline, Balzac had devoted himself more determinedly to work on *Le Médecin de Campagne*. He went into one of his periods of very intensive writing. Often, after a short period of sleep, he would work through the night from one till eight o'clock, drink some coffee, and then continue working until about four o'clock in the afternoon. He worked on the novel for about a year, from September 1832 to September 1833. It finally appeared in the shops in September 1833, just a few weeks before he set off for his first meeting with Mme Hanska. Balzac wrote and re-wrote, greatly modifying his original draft. He intended it to be considered a highly moral book, and, in a letter to Eveline, described it as an updated version of *The Imitation of Christ*. The novel tells the story of a doctor who attempts to educate the people of a mountain village and bring them into the modern world. It was put on the short list for the Prix Montyon, which was awarded every year for literature considered to be virtuous in intent. But it was eventually awarded second place, and the critics found it rather dull and dogmatic.

In the middle of 1833, Balzac also worked on another idea which was to be a forerunner of his all-embracing *La Comédie humaine*. He gave it the general title of *Études de Moeurs au XIXe Siècle*. It was to include all his novels and stories divided into four series, which can be translated as *Scenes of Private*, *Provincial*, *Parisian* and *Country Life*. This way of thinking about his work, with each part contributing to a greater whole, undoubtedly gave him the courage and energy to continue working. This is also the reason why, from this stage of his life onwards, Balzac spent a lot of his time revising already published work. To check earlier works for errors he even employed a proofreader, who found, to Balzac's distress, that there were many. Balzac even involved Laure's two children, ten and twelve years old, in checking his works for grammatical mistakes: when they found one, they had to mark the page with a little cross.

A bizarre incident occurred early in August. Louis Mame decided to take Balzac to court: he had quite simply lost patience with waiting for the final text of *Le Médecin de Campagne*. Balzac wanted it printed in one volume the size of a prayer book and Mame refused. Balzac lost the case and was ordered to deliver the manuscript as agreed. Then, while an appeal was under way, Balzac vented his anger in a more physical way. He went to his old printing works early in the morning at about six o'clock and was let into the building by his old partner Barbier. He then spent the entire day damaging and generally spoiling the printing blocks for the novel, thereby preventing the book from being printed.

Another publisher, Louise Béchet, agreed to publish his *Études de Moeurs* in an edition of twelve volumes, and Balzac was able to take up work again on the novel *Eugénie Grandet* (1833). This tells the story of the devotion of Eugénie to her cousin Charles. Although her father forbids it, she helps the ne'er-do-well relative by giving him her collection of gold coins. The ironical twist in the novel is that the unselfish daughter eventually starts to acquire some of the attributes of her father.

Another remarkable work of this period which merits special mention is the story 'L'Illustre Gaudissart'. Gaudissart, an ugly caricature of a man, travels in the Touraine region selling life insurance. In the town of Vouvray a local man, for the sheer fun of it, advises him to call on one house, where, unbeknownst to Gaudissart, a madman lives. The rest of the story is a brilliantly devised dialogue in which each man conducts one side of what he thinks is a completely logical conversation, but they are in fact discussing two different topics. The origin of the story is amusing in itself. The printer had chosen a rather small font for one of the volumes of the *Scènes de la Vie de Province*, and this left eighty blank pages to be filled. Balzac wrote down the story of about

14,000 words, about Gaudissart, which may have been gestating in his mind for some time, within one single night.

Just before Christmas 1833, Balzac went to Geneva again. This time he stayed in a hotel called the Auberge de l'Arc, quite close to where Mme Hanska and her husband were living in the district called Pré-Lévêque. There were many pleasant social occasions and some secret meetings between the two lovers in Balzac's hotel. On 26th January 1834, it seems that they were particularly intimate, though there is no record of what actually happened. There were also clear indications that Eveline would be willing to marry Balzac after her husband, who was not in good health, had died.

After about six and a half weeks of sharing their exhilarating love, Balzac returned to Paris in early February 1834. In a letter to his sister Laure, he revealed some startling news at this time: he had become a father. The identity of the child was kept secret for a long time, and it is not even certain if the child in question was Balzac's. He, however, clearly believed himself to be its father. Although not incontrovertible, there is some evidence indicating who the mother was, and what name the child bore. There is a reference to a certain 'Maria' in the dedication of *Eugénie Grandet* and it seems likely that this refers to Maria du Fresnay. The nephew of the child in question has confirmed that among the papers of Maria du Fresnay there was a copy of the second edition of *Eugénie Grandet* in which the dedication to 'Maria' first appeared. The child was called Maria-Caroline and must have been conceived in September 1833 before Balzac left for Neuchâtel. She was born in Sartrouville on 4th June 1834. The nephew recalled being told by his aunt that Balzac frequently came to see her and also attended her first communion.

That same spring, Balzac went to visit Issodoun, about 140 miles south of Paris. Zulma Carraud and her husband had moved to her father's estate on François-Michel's retirement. Balzac had two rooms to himself at one end of the house. While staying with them he developed ideas for the work entitled *Mémoires de Deux Jeunes Mariées*. This would not be published until 1842, but it reveals many influences of this period at Issodoun, when Zulma was pregnant with her second child and Balzac was generally obsessed with babies.

In June 1834, Balzac's younger brother Henry suddenly appeared out of the blue. He had come back from working in the colonies, where he had acquired a wife, who was now pregnant, and a stepson. Balzac had plans to get rid of him again by sending him off to work as a trader in the Indian Ocean. As an experienced town-planner Henry was responsible for designing the capital of Réunion but he ended up working as a surveyor and died in 1858.

That spring Mme de Berny was not in good health. She was in her fifty-ninth year and had serious heart problems. She had gone through trying times with her children: her son was dying, another daughter had been sent to an asylum, and a third would die in July. Balzac noticed that she had aged enormously. During his last stay with her at La Bouleaunière in October 1835, he read to her his novel *Le Lys dans la Vallée*. After this meeting, Mme de Berny told him that it would be best if they did not meet again. She was to die in July 1836, while Balzac was travelling to Italy.

It is not certain when exactly Balzac conceived the basic plan of *La Comédie humaine*. Laure claimed that it was at the time of the publication of *Le Médecin de Campagne* (at the end of 1833) but *Le Père Goriot* (which appeared in instalments at the end of 1834) is the first work which he attempted to fit into the scheme and which follows its basic principles. The organising theme was a blindingly simple one which exhilarated Balzac when he discovered it. He suddenly realised that the same characters could reappear in different novels and a whole complex interrelated universe of people and events could be created. Once he decided on this grand scheme of things he set about making the necessary modifications to his existing works and to plans for future works. The first connecting links were established by adding characters to works in which they did not figure prominently.

They might be mentioned or referred to in some way in dialogues. *Le Père Goriot* was the first work to make use of the system extensively. There were twenty-three characters in the first edition who would reappear in other works, and in later editions the figure would rise to forty-eight. As a result, Balzac found it necessary to draw up detailed family trees. Despite these interconnections, each of the works, story or novel, can be read in isolation, and the meaning of no one work is dependent on knowledge of another. In such a mammoth undertaking there are naturally enough inconsistencies: one that is often mentioned is the fact that the Baron de Maulincour is poisoned by Ferragus in the middle of 1919 but is being admired by Eugène-Louis de Rastignac in November of that same year. And there are many others, some only small details, such as the colour of eyes or hair.

In the latter part of 1835, as well as working on *Le Père Goriot*, Balzac worked on *La Recherche de l'Absolu*, in which an obsessive scientist destroys his family's fortune in the search for ultimate scientific principles, and also the story of 'Séraphita', which is set in the fjords of Norway and tells of the metamorphosis of a strange creature, a kind of angel who is half woman and half man.

It is in *Le Pére Goriot* that Balzac's arch-villain, Jacques Collin, alias Vautrin, appears. This character was inspired by Balzac's meeting with an infamous convict who had become a detective and eventually head of the Sûreté, a certain François Vidocq. It is known that Balzac attended a dinner at which Vidocq was also present. It seems that he enjoyed his company and admired his powers of detection. In one significant aspect, however, Vidocq differed from his fictional counterpart. It was known that Vidocq hated homosexuals, but there is clearly a homosexual component in Vautrin's relationship with Rastignac in *Le Père Goriot*. This could of course be mischievous irony on the part of Balzac, but psychoanalytical theory also suggests that excessive hatred of homosexuals is likely to stem from repression of similar tendencies. Speculation has always been rife about Balzac's own relationships with the young men he took under his wing in this period of his life. There was, for example, the twenty-three-year-old Jules Sandeau, who was handsome and easily impressed and was taken on by Balzac as his secretary when rejected as a lover by George Sand. Sandeau had attempted suicide before Balzac invited him to come and live with him. But Sandeau could not stand the regime that Balzac had envisioned for him: that he was to write books guided by Balzac. He soon left what he clearly felt was a suffocating atmosphere. At the end of 1835, Balzac took on two new male assistants: Ferdinand de Grammont and Auguste de Belloy. Though they helped him in various minor ways (Belloy helped with the plot of the short story 'Gambara'), Balzac clearly felt that they too were not of the mettle he desired. Meanwhile, Mme Hanska and the Duchesse d'Abrantès were clearly both suspicious of his relationships with these young men, especially with Sandeau, and there is evidence, in the correspondence, of Balzac being aware of feminine, maternal and indeed androgynous aspects of his own personality. In a letter to Mme Hanska he attempts to reassure her about rumours of his womanising by expressing an intention to flirt only with men.[10]

This period of 'flirting' with young men coincided with Balzac turning himself into more of a dandy. He became a collector of a large number of fancy waistcoats and other decorative baubles, including an elaborate walking stick, for which he became famous. It had a large golden knob, was encrusted with turquoise and hung with tassels. Despite all these self-indulgences and socialising, he was able to spend on average at least eighteen hours a day writing. In March 1835, he decided that he needed some kind of sanctuary to which he could retreat and cut himself off from the world. He rented a house in the quiet suburb of Chaillot, at 13 Rue des Batailles. It was small and rundown but had a superb view of the Seine and the whole of central Paris. Balzac instructed builders to create a completely soundproofed boudoir, which was to be lavishly decorated with a chandelier and marble figures, imitation silk wallpaper, and rugs. This retreat was not purely for purposes of literary creation: it was a way of escaping from the growing number of his creditors. To protect himself and ensure that undesirables could not gain access, Balzac devised a number of passwords, which had to be uttered before anyone was allowed in. It seems, however, that he still did not feel completely secure in this hideaway, as he is known to have stayed at an unknown address at Meudon, in the woods to the west of Paris, during April and May in 1835, when he was finishing his story 'La Fille aux Yeux d'Or' (to be included in *Histoire des Treize*), and the preface for the second edition of *Le Père Goriot*.

On 9th May Balzac set off for Vienna, for a meeting with Eveline. Though he spent much of his visit writing, he was also introduced through Eveline to several persons of note, including the Chancellor Metternich and General Prinz Schwarzenberg. He left Vienna on 4th June and passed through Munich on his way back to Paris.

On arrival in Paris, Balzac was met with yet more paternity rumours. While attending receptions at the Austrian embassy in Paris, Balzac had met and developed a strong liking for an English woman named Frances Sarah Lovell, born on a large estate near Malmesbury in Wiltshire. Her husband was a rather dull inattentive Italian nobleman, Count Emilio Guidoboni-Visconti. She and Mme Hanska had common acquaintances and Eveline was soon complaining to Balzac about the rumours she had heard. It is known from incontestable evidence (receipts for the hiring of coaches) that Balzac travelled to Versailles where the Countess had a summer home, and to Boulogne at times when it is known that she was travelling to and from England. On one occasion Balzac stayed in Boulogne for a week. When, nine months later, Frances had a son, it was christened Lionel after her other lover, the Comte de Bonneval, but there was a strong rumour that the father was Balzac. Reading between the lines of his denials in his letters to Eveline, it is possible to believe that Balzac might have been the father.

Debtor, Entrepreneur and Playwright
1836–42

By 1836, Balzac was showing clear signs of ageing. His hair was starting to turn grey and to fall out, and he had to resort to the use of a toupee. He suffered from frequent inflammation of the blood vessels around the brain, and often had pains down his right side. In the middle of 1836, while at Saché, he had what was probably a mild stroke. He reported buzzing sounds in his head and occasional loss of balance. He also had regular attacks of back and chest pains and bronchitis. He was depressed by both his physical and clearly related dull mental state. He started to become obsessed with how much time he had left and how much time he would need to complete his magnum opus. None of this however seems to have made him slow down the pace of his writing.

In the years 1836 and 1837, Balzac turned out four novels: *La Vieille Fille*, *Les Employés*, *L'Interdiction*, and *César Birotteau* (the well-known story of a seller of hair-restorer who becomes bankrupt). There were also more contributions to the *Contes Drolatiques*, several short stories and plans and sketches for other works, including *Illusions Perdues*. On top of this came his journalistic output and all the correcting of proofs, which was a truly time-consuming job, not only for Balzac, but for his printers who had to decipher all his scrawlings. His motivation was, as ever, not only artistic but to try and get on top of his debts at long last.

Balzac had other plans to solve his enormous debt problems. One involved him in the purchase of a six-eighths share in a weekly magazine, the *Chronique de Paris*, founded in 1834 by William Duckett, a businessman of Irish origin. When Balzac bought his share on Christmas Eve 1835, he also agreed to underwrite all expenses. The original aims of the publication were to encourage and support young writers and to be impartial in the choice and judgement of works. Balzac had other plans: he wanted to use the magazine as his own private vehicle, for the publication of his own works, thus avoiding what he considered to be exploitation by his editors. Balzac was particularly sensitive to such issues at the time: he was in the process of taking the *Revue de Paris* to court for having sold the uncorrected proofs of his novel *Le Lys dans la Vallée* to a magazine in St Petersburg. On 4th June 1836, the court found in his favour.

Meanwhile, Balzac insisted that the *Chronique de Paris* should appear twice weekly, and in the period from February to July 1836 he wrote forty-one editorials, many of which were in favour of stronger ties with Russia rather than England (one suspects that his own personal hopes for the future may have influenced his judgement somewhat). He estimated that he spent up to thirty-six hours twice a week working on the magazine.

On 27th April there was a remarkable interlude. Balzac had for a long time successfully avoided doing his National Guard Duty, which obliged citizens to spend one night on sentry duty, but on this day the law caught up with him. He was thrown into prison for seven days. Conditions in the prison were awful. It was unpleasantly cold and he kept company with the lowest of the low. He came out of prison to find that William Duckett had sensed that the magazine would not survive and quit. Balzac tried to get financial support to save it, but it finally collapsed in July. Its demise was undoubtedly hastened by the advent of cheap daily newspapers which presented their political views with greater clarity and conviction. Balzac had to bear the losses to the shareholders himself. He felt that the illusions he had held about his future in journalism had been shattered.

There is a clear connection between Balzac's own situation and the inspiration he had for a novel while staying in Saché during this period. It was to be about a man called Lucien de Rubempré who is drawn into the world of journalism and succumbs to corruption. In a later novel he was to fall victim to the arch-villain Vautrin. The novel which was conceived in Saché was *Illusions Perdues*.

Balzac made another attempt to control the whole process of publishing his novels through the publisher Edmond Werdet. For some time the agreement seemed likely to work. Balzac managed to persuade Werdet to give him very large advances, but also he rather thoughtlessly signed many promissory notes benefiting Werdet. The novels published by Werdet sold very well, but this did not prevent Werdet from going bankrupt in May 1837. Balzac then had to honour all the promissory notes he had issued, but he did that with the aid of advances from yet another publisher. Werdet's subsequent career went from bad to worse: he went bankrupt again in 1845, turned to working as a travelling salesman, and ended his life miserably, having been crippled in an accident, gone blind and lost both wife and property.

Meanwhile, Balzac's feelings for Sarah, wife of the Count Visconti, were becoming more intense. Her mother-in-law died and she asked Balzac to help her protect her husband's inheritance. On 25th July 1836, Balzac set off for Italy, arriving at Turin after five days travelling, where he was received with enthusiasm in the local salons. He was accompanied on this trip by a young woman called Caroline Marbouty. She came from Limoges, where her father was a magistrate and her brother a clerk of the court, and had aspirations to be a writer. She had two stories accepted by Balzac for the *Chronique de Paris* and later had some success as a feminist writer. To accompany Balzac to Italy she dressed herself as a man, and, not surprisingly, was frequently mistaken for George Sand. It seems likely that Balzac and she had a short passionate affair: the return journey to France took them much longer than expected, and they spent an exceptionally long time in Switzerland together. They rarely met again after this trip.

Around this time, Émile de Girardin, owner of the daily newspaper, *La Presse*, the appearance of which had contributed to the collapse of the *Chronique de Paris*, invited Balzac to write a novel which would be serialised in his paper. Balzac agreed and sent him *La Vieille Fille*. It was published in twelve daily episodes, starting on 23rd October 1836, and was the first novel to be serialised in this way (as a so-called *roman feuilleton*) in France. However, Balzac was never really happy with the process of writing in this way: of having to keep things simple and to avoid controversial topics, as well as contriving suspense for the end of each episode. Many readers also protested about Balzac's theme of the sexual frustrations of an old woman. But it seems that the interest aroused by the work did at least help to boost the sales of the newspaper.

In an article in *Revue de Deux Mondes*, the author Saint-Beuve revealed a fact that most people had either conveniently forgotten or had never known: that Balzac had earlier published various works under the pseudonym of Lord R'Hoone. Balzac turned the disclosure to his own advantage and did a deal with the publisher Hippolyte Souverain to republish the works in question, modified somewhat and tidied up. Despite also signing another contract for all his future works which brought him an advance of 50,000 francs, Balzac was still deeply in debt and was constantly avoiding his creditors. To circumvent the bailiffs he had to move all his furniture from the Rue Cassini to the Rue des Batailles. When this new address was discovered, he pretended to move to the Rue de Provence, to fool his pursuers. But early in February 1837, the bailiffs managed to take possession of his carriage from the Rue Cassini.

Sarah Visconti needed help sorting out her husband's affairs again, and on 14th February, Balzac set out for Italy again, this time alone. On the 19th, he arrived in Milan and took a room in one of the best hotels, near La Scala theatre. Another acquaintance, the Countess Sanseverino, arranged for him to be loaned the private coach of her brother, Prince Porcia, and also allowed him access to the Prince's private box at La Scala. He was introduced to the famous author of *I Promessi Sposi*, Alessandro Manzoni, but they did not get on, with Balzac talking about himself most of the time. He also attended the salon of the twenty-three-year-old Countess Maffei, to whom he subsequently wrote in very flattering terms, while staying in Venice on an errand related to Count Visconti's affairs. Countess Maffei's husband became aware of Balzac's attentions to his wife and warned her off in no uncertain terms.

Balzac spent the next month in Italy, visiting Livorno, Bologna, where he met Rossini, and Florence. He set off from Milan on his return journey to France on 24th April 1837. On his return, he learned of the death of Mme de Berny, and on doctor's orders, took to his bed for three whole days to overcome his grief. When he had recovered, he wrote to Mme Hanska of his plans for literary production: to publish *César Birotteau*, 'La Femme Supérieure' and 'Gambara', and to finish writing 'La Haute Banque', 'Les Artistes' and *Illusions Perdues*. Balzac also considered writing more plays.

However, Balzac's creditors still allowed him no peace, and so he sought sanctuary in the Paris home of the Viscontis, in the Avenue des Champs-Elysées. Even here he was not safe. William Duckett had obtained a court order against him and a bailiff disguised as a mail delivery man went to the Viscontis' house, asking to see M. de Balzac to obtain his signature for a parcel. The parcel proved to contain papers demanding that Balzac pay 3,000 francs immediately or he would be sent to prison. The Viscontis settled the debt for him.

Despite such setbacks and the threat of more, Balzac decided to stay in Paris, and obtained some land in an area to the south-west of the city, beyond the Porte Saint-Cloud. One of its merits was that it was outside the jurisdiction of the National Guard. Balzac planned to have a house built there and already had a name for his retreat: 'Les Jardies'.

In the period between February 1836 and the middle of 1837, Balzac frequently felt that Mme Hanska was starting to become too critical of him in a manner reminiscent of his mother, and he turned to another correspondent whom he knew only as 'Louise'. Much has been speculated about the identity of this woman, but it is difficult to reach any firm conclusions. In summary, the facts are as follows. The magazine *La Mode* announced, ten months after Balzac's death, in June 1851, the publication of twenty-three letters from Balzac to a society lady, 'Louise'. Mme Hanska took out an injunction against the publisher. The letters were to appear eventually in the collected correspondence in 1876, with one more letter appearing at a later date. The most likely candidate for the woman known as 'Louise' would appear to be a young actress calling herself professionally Atala Beauchêne, who was born Louise-Agathe Beaudoin in Orléans in 1819. In one of the letters she admits that 'Louise' is one of her real names but not the one she was generally known by. She is also known to have been present at a dinner attended by Balzac. Atala Beauchêne moved in the same circles as some of Balzac's friends and later he was to ask for her to be given a part in one of his plays. After his return from Milan, the correspondence gradually came to an end, but with good feelings on both sides. He dedicated the story 'Facino Cane' (1836) to her, but then, for some reason, removed it at a later date. He also asked her never to reveal her true identity.

In order to observe progress on his new property, 'Les Jardies', and also to keep at bay, as ever, his creditors, Balzac bought an apartment in nearby Sèvres. For a long time it was just a muddy construction site, with a few sheds and other small buildings, but in Balzac's imagination it was a charming arbour draped in climbing plants. He also had plans to convert the old stables into a cowshed so that he could sell dairy products in the local area.

Later he was also to develop a scheme for accumulating manure and selling it to the local farmers. There would be a vegetable garden too, not to mention a lake, a vineyard and a pineapple plantation, and poplars, magnolias and linden trees. The house which was built for Balzac on the site eventually had three stories with two rooms on each floor, and one of the rooms on the top floor was his study with superb views over the woods of Versailles in one direction and over Sèvres in the other. Balzac sketched on the walls in charcoal outlines of the objects he wanted to have there, though none of them materialised: a Delacroix, a Rembrandt, a Titian, a Raphaël. But he was not just daydreaming; he was working too: on *Les Paysans*, begun at this time, published in part in 1844, but never finished.

However, no sooner had Balzac settled in 'Les Jardies' than another obsession gripped him, at the end of 1837, which was to lead to one of the most reckless, potentially dangerous undertakings of his life. Balzac would seek his fortune pursuing a dream, which if fulfilled might well lead him to abandon literature altogether – such was the tone in which he was writing to Mme Hanska at the time. And while making his fortune he would also enjoy solitude, and commune with Nature. Before setting off on this enterprise Balzac went to visit Zulma Carraud in the spring of 1838 and followed this with a farewell visit to George Sand.

Balzac's imagination had been fired by something he had learned from a businessman, when in Genoa. The man told him of ancient silver mines in Sardinia which had been worked by the Romans but then left to go derelict. Balzac convinced himself that with the aid of modern technology it must be possible to extract more silver from the site. After very inadequate research he set off. At that time Sardinia was a wild, inhospitable island, with hordes of marauding bandits. On the journey he kept a journal which was basically a collection of letters he planned to send to Eveline.

It took him four days of travelling through Provence, with little food to sustain him, to reach Marseille. Here he was fêted by local writers and spent some time browsing in local antique shops. From here, he went to the port of Toulon, and took a steamboat for Ajaccio in Corsica, where due to fears of cholera he was quarantined from 23rd March to 4th April. He found little to distract him there, and even a visit to a run-down old shack which was reputed to be the birthplace of Napoleon was only a disappointment. His only solace was that no one recognised him and he was left in peace; until a local student realised who he was and wrote a report on his presence for the local paper. Balzac finally set off for Sardinia on a boat fishing for coral which was heading for Africa. It was a very uncomfortable journey, on which he was forced to eat fish soup every day, and finally had to spend another five days in quarantine and moored in a storm off Alghiero in Sardinia. Some details of his subsequent travels cannot be confirmed, but it seems that on the advice of locals he set off on horseback towards the mountains of Argentiera in the north-west part of the island. Here he gathered some rock samples and returned to Alghiero, but set off immediately again into the wildest part of the interior. It is likely that he reached Iglesias in the south-west part and managed to visit the old mines called Domus Novas. Then he went back to Alghiero again and set off yet again for Sassari, from where it was possible to take a coach to Cagliari. From here he eventually sailed back to Italy on 17th April. But on arrival in Cagliari Balzac received some bad news: the businessman he had met in Genoa had decided to pursue the dream himself, obtained a mining licence and become a partner of a company based in Marseille, with the aim of exploring the mines. There was nothing left for Balzac to do but make his way back to Paris via Italy. Although he continued to dream of treasure-hunting over the next few years, including a vaguely formulated plan to go to Brazil, his creative endeavours on returning to Paris were focused on writing plays.

This was also a time when the state of politics in France was of great concern to Balzac, a concern which is reflected in some of his writing. For example, in 'Z. Marcas' (first published in 1840), an elderly political genius reflects on the fact that the young people of his day feel that their political ambitions are thwarted by the way in which the older generation cling to power. There are intimations in this work of the revolution which would eventually destroy the so-called 'bourgeois monarchy' in 1848. In 1839, there were already violent protests – which were brutally repressed. Balzac felt that the government had reacted clumsily and insensitively. This unruly situation did not drive Balzac to the left in his political sympathies however; rather he turned more to the right. One reason for this was that he perceived the Liberal factions as being just as repressive, especially in regard to the issue of free speech. He had direct experience of this in his own dealings with the leftwing publication *Le Siècle*, which refused to publish one of his articles out of fear of offending those members of society whom he was criticising.

As with all his undertakings, Balzac went at his bout of playwriting in this period with great gusto, but none of the plays were commercial successes. The first of them was *L'École des Ménages*, about a shopkeeper who is married but falls in love with his head sales-girl. Its combination of realism and farce did not appeal to the Renaissance Theatre, to which Balzac offered the play, and they turned it down. It is interesting to note that Balzac was helped in his writing of this play by another of his young protégés, a poor poet called Charles Lassailly. The play was not performed until 1910. The next play Balzac wrote utilised the arch-criminal character from his novels, and bore the character's name as its title: *Vautrin*. This story of a clever criminal who manages to pass himself off as a member of high society lacked the subtlety of his counterpart in the novels. Balzac dreamed of writing the play together with a large group of assistants, but this did not happen, and the only co-writer was a man known as Laurent-Jan, who remained a devoted friend of Balzac. The play opened in the Saint-Martin Theatre to a packed audience on 14th March 1840. Audience and critics alike found it difficult to decide what kind of play it was: a tragedy, comedy, or perhaps a political satire? Whatever it was, it was banned the next day. It has never been clear why this happened: perhaps it was perceived as a political satire, or perhaps some powerful individual felt himself lampooned in the play.

Balzac also became involved in a cause célèbre in which he felt that an injustice had been perpetrated. This was the so-called Peytel affair. The facts of the case as described by the man accused were as follows. In the small town of Belley, near the Swiss border, in the night of 1st November 1838, a young solicitor named Sébastien Peytel woke up the local magistrate and doctor. His wife lay dead in their carriage. According to Peytel, they were returning from Mâcon with a large sum of money. Their servant suddenly stopped the coach and shot Mme Peytel, killing her. Peytel pursued him and struck him with a hammer (he was an amateur geologist and had a hammer with him), smashing his skull in the process. The court did not believe his story, and became convinced that he had murdered both his wife and the servant. Peytel was duly sentenced to death in the assizes at Bourg on 30th August 1839.

Balzac, who had known Peytel in the early 1830s when the younger man had some success writing theatre reviews, decided to try to help him. He interviewed him in prison and went to visit the scene of the incident. Returning to Paris, he wrote a 'Lettre sur le Procès de Peytel', which was published in three national newspapers. Balzac's defence of Peytel was cleverly contrived, revealing how the court had only really considered evidence which was unfavourable to the accused. There was one piece of evidence which Balzac had to conceal, however, in order to argue in Peytel's favour. This evidence demonstrates that it was in all likelihood a crime of passion which Peytel himself had tried to cover up: his wife had been having an affair with the servant. In all likelihood, Peytel left the carriage for a few moments, returning to find his wife and the servant in an intimate situation. He shot his wife and bludgeoned the servant to death. Even though Balzac doubtless knew these facts he clearly felt that his friend did not deserve to die because the murders were not premeditated. Balzac's open letter was ahead of its time in its condemnation of the cavalier handling of forensic evidence. But Balzac's efforts were to no avail. Although the king was known to be considering commuting the sentence to hard labour, he received a letter reminding him of the detrimental effects if he were to grant an acquittal, and Peytel was guillotined on 28th October 1839. Balzac was angry but helpless. His fury would colour his opinion of the judicial system for many years to come.

There were two stories published in 1839 which were closely based on facts, and which can be described as *romans à clé*: 'Béatrix' and 'Les Secrets de la Princesse de Cadignan'. The former was based on Franz Liszt's affair with Marie d'Agoult, and the latter on the affair between the Comtesse de Castellane and Count Molé, the Minister for Foreign Affairs. It is likely that the sensationalist aspects of these stories were related to the fact that his works were now almost entirely published first in newspapers and such themes would have appealed very much to a majority of the readers.

In July 1840, Balzac made his second attempt at founding a review. He got the idea from another publication which had recently proved to be very popular. It was a pocket-sized magazine called *Les Guêlpes*. Balzac's was called the *Revue Parisienne*, and it was so small and compact that many readers complained that it was impossible to read. It dealt with political and social issues, such as workers' riots, working conditions in industry, and poor housing. Balzac's own contributions clearly reveal him to be right of centre politically. He abhorred riots and demonstrations and favoured a powerful head of state of some kind. But the review ran to only three issues. In September 1840, Armand Dutacq, who had originally helped Balzac set it up, withdrew from the enterprise, and after that there was no way in which it could survive. Balzac had at least managed to publish two of his stories in the review: 'Z. Marcas' and 'Un Prince de la Bohème'.

It is at about this time that Balzac decided on the general, collective title for his literary output. He first mentioned the concept of *La Comédie humaine* in a letter to a publisher in January 1840. It may have been coined by another writer or poet friend, but its precise origin is not known. Its ironical allusion to Dante's *Divine Comedy* was clearly intended from the start.

By now things were not going well at Balzac's property, 'Les Jardies'. There had been some serious storm damage and his creditors had tracked down the address. Finally Balzac decided to move all his furniture to the small house he had set aside there for the use of the Viscontis, so that the bailiffs would find nothing in his own house that they could legally remove. But at the end of 1840 he had to sell the entire property and he now rented a small house in Passy, in the far western part of Paris. It was conveniently located between an upper and a lower road, so that if creditors came to one door he could escape through the other. He started to work on a new play, which was to be a comedy, entitled *Mercadet*, and concerned the tricks a man uses to avoid his creditors.

Correspondence with Mme Hanska did not exactly flourish in the three years from 1839 to 1841, and Balzac found himself tempted into an affair with a rich widow called Hélène de Valette. She had written to him under her maiden name after reading the story 'Béatrix', which contains a description of the area where she lived in Brittany. In a letter to Mme Hanska, Balzac mentions a trip to Brittany in the late spring of 1841, when, presumably, he could have met up with Mme de Valette. It was a brief affair, which ended before the end of the year. Nothing was heard of the woman again until after Balzac died when she tried to blackmail Mme Hanska with threats to publish her correspondence with Balzac. There is also evidence of casual affairs of an even shorter duration in this period.

Soon after moving into the house in Passy, Balzac did a rather rash and surprising thing: he invited his mother to come and stay with him, giving her one hundred francs a month as spending money and providing her with a companion and a maid. He wrote to his sister Laure, asking her to deal with all the arrangements. The experiment lasted little more than a year and a half. Mother and son spent a lot of the time complaining about each other.

In 1842, Balzac published what is essentially his one significant theoretical work on literature – that is to say, on his own contribution to literature. It was a labour that he did not particularly want to undertake, but no one else was willing to do so, and so he set about explaining exactly what his aims were in his Preface to *La Comédie humaine* in 1842. In it, he compares human types to animal species and posits that all creatures developed from a single original entity (comparable to Goethe's *Urpflanze* in the plant world), which, under the influence of environment, diversified into manifold forms. Passion has always been a destructive force in creation, while society exerts a positive moulding force. The regulating and stabilising forces in society are monarchy and religious institutions. In his writing Balzac wanted to describe the lives of a few thousand prominent and influential individuals. While this sums up adequately his views at the time of writing, it is generally agreed that the prescriptions in the Preface do not fit easily all the works he produced. Individual works can be perceived to jar against the framework he stipulated. Some of the later novels, in particular, belie his emphasis in the Preface on the positive role of the family in society.

To Russia With Love
1842–50

On 5th January 1842, Balzac received a letter, which determined the direction of the rest of his life: it announced that Eveline's husband, Wenceslas Hanski, had died on 10th November 1841. There was now no barrier, or so it seemed, to marrying Eveline and finding true happiness. Balzac wrote to her, declaring that he would come to join her in Russia as soon as he had regulated his affairs. He even considered applying for Russian citizenship. And he dreamed of starting a magazine on European themes based in St Petersburg. He visualised the second half of his life as being spent devoted to her: he was almost forty-three and she in her mid-thirties, so they had the beautiful prospect of growing old together before them.

Eveline, however, was not yet sure about the path her life should take in the future and what role Honoré should play in it. It was seven years since they had last seen each other. Her own diary for this period, kept in French, reveals some aspects of her concerns. Her husband's ailing old cousin was attempting to obtain an injunction to prevent Wenceslas' estate ending up in Balzac's hands. Even without the cousin's intervention, there was still no certainty that Eveline, who was neither a member of the Orthodox church nor Russian by birth, would inherit. Balzac channelled all his anxieties and worries into a very autobiographical novel called *Albert Savarus* (1842), the central character of which, like Balzac, has worries that his work and political activities may have all been a waste of time. In September 1842, Eveline went to live in St Petersburg partly in order that she could follow the progress of the court case concerning the inheritance. While there, she became subject to the amorous attentions of the elderly Comte de Balk, who had once been a lover of the eminent writer Mme De Staël. A more challenging rival to the affections of Balzac was the pianist and composer Franz Liszt, whom Eveline met through a letter of introduction which Balzac had written himself. Liszt clearly decided to attempt to seduce her and put on his usual vehemently romantic performances both at the piano and in his declarations of love. She was not to be won over, however, and at their last meeting on 3rd June 1843, she firmly declined his offer of love, reassuring him that of course it would be impossible to forget a man like him.

Before eventually setting off to St Petersburg, Balzac spent an extraordinarily productive period, writing numerous stories, including two which he remained especially proud of: 'Honorine' and 'Le Curé de Village'. He also began work on *L'Envers de l'Histoire Contemporaine*, about a secret organisation devoted to performing acts of charity.

Apart from his letters to Eveline, there are few other letters by Balzac of any significant length extant from the period from 1842 to 1845. The most common recipients are publishers, and his solicitor, Pierre Gavault, who was also one of the rare visitors to Balzac's house in Passy at that time. In order to cover his tracks and confuse his creditors, Balzac had arranged for the lease of his house to be signed by a certain Philiberte-Louise Breugnol. All letters to him were to be addressed to a M. Breugnol, who did not in fact exist. There was a woman with a similar sounding name: Louise Breugniot. She was Balzac's housekeeper for about five years. She continued to dress in a style which betrayed her origins in the countryside of the Massif Central area. Although Balzac may never have intended it, it seems that Louise built up some expectations of one day becoming his mistress and even of their ending their days together. Whatever the truth of the matter, their relationship was clearly more than just that of master and servant. Her hopes were finally dashed when the letter announcing Wenceslas Hanski's death arrived.

On the evening of 19th March 1842, Balzac experienced the disastrous first night of the play he had written and entitled *Les Resources de Quinolla*. It was on the theme of how great inventors and original thinkers frequently have their ambitious and inspired plans scuttled by envious and small-minded people and, especially, by creditors. The nautical metaphor was central to the play: in the sixteenth century a man invents a steamboat but out of exasperation at the obstructions he encounters to his plan, he decides to sink his prototype in the harbour of Barcelona. Reviewers saw clearly that the real subject of the play was Balzac's own struggles with his creditors. Apart from the actors who actually appeared on the stage, the production was virtually a one-man show: Balzac controlled everything. He led the first read-through, with only four of the five acts complete, improvising the final act on the spot. He directed rehearsals, correcting and changing the text all the time, and also sat in the box office selling tickets at exorbitant prices and only to people he considered to be of suitable social standing. As it turned out, the house was only about a quarter full on the first night. The play was booed and the actors pelted by whatever the audience had to hand. The play somehow survived for nineteen nights and was not performed again until 1863. The behaviour of the audience was not exceptional for the time, and Balzac himself clearly did not regard it as an unmitigated disaster. He realised that many members of the audience came with the intention of not liking the play and caused a furore just because the work was by him.

Before leaving for Russia in June 1843, Balzac indulged in what can only be described as a writing and printing binge: for about a month or so he actually lived in a printing works in Lagny, north-east of Paris. Here, together with twenty workers, he toiled away, for nineteen hours a day, checking and correcting pages as soon as they came off the presses, handing them back to be reprinted and writing the next part of the novel while awaiting the next set of proofs. In this way he finished the third part of *Illusions Perdues* and the first part of *Splendeurs et Misères des Courtisanes*.

After having settled at least some of his debts, Balzac left Paris on 19th July to undertake a nine-day sea voyage to St Petersburg. He and Eveline met again at last in her house at midday on 29th July. Since the early 1830s, Balzac's novels had become famous in Russia through translations, and as a result of his fame and her influence they were able to attend a review of the Imperial Guard. Balzac even managed to see the Tsar. Eveline and he discussed plans for a visit to Paris together, strolled along the banks of the Neva, and he read to her from his novels. By the time Balzac finally left St Petersburg early in October, he was not in good health, and had to endure a rather depressing journey overland to France.

A young Russian sculptor, N.A. Ramazanov, shared Balzac's coach with him for a large part of the journey. The sculptor kept a diary, in which he noted vivid images of Balzac, and recorded many of his comments and opinions on the places they were travelling through and the people they met. Finally, on 14th October, they reached Berlin and the two wandered round the city observing the sights. They made short trips to Dresden and Leipzig, and met various celebrities, including Alexander von Humboldt.

There is a mysterious gap in Balzac's itinerary between 21st October, when he was definitely in Dresden, and 3rd November, when he was back in Paris. It has been assumed that he travelled up the Rhine from Mainz to Cologne and then through Belgium, but the biographer Graham Robb argues that this is the only possible time when Balzac could have met up with his housekeeper Louise Breugniot, travelled south with her and visited the house in Baden-Baden which she was later to revisit.[11]

After his return to Paris, Balzac's health took a turn for the worse. His head problems (arachnoiditis) were treated with leeches and he was given external applications of opium for neuralgia. He was also beset by other afflictions, including jaundice, colds and what was probably another mild stroke in February 1844, after which he coughed blood for some time.

In the meantime, Eveline had at last won her court case and the two were planning for her to visit Paris secretly. She was not allowed a passport to France however, so they agreed that she would travel on Balzac's passport, with Eveline pretending to be his sister and Anna his niece. They would meet up in Dresden.

By the end of 1845, Balzac had managed to pay off a considerable number of his debts, though by no means all. The methods he had used were not exactly legal: borrowing further money under assumed names, getting friends who owed him nothing to sign promissory notes, and pretending to be much poorer than he actually was. Eventually, Eveline would begin to pay off his debts and pay for all their other indulgences, such as holidays. She could not commit herself to marrying him, however, as she still had several worries connected with the estate. This in itself would not necessarily provide sufficient income for them both, and it was still uncertain if she would be allowed to keep the estate if she married a foreigner. One solution would be if she could marry off her daughter, Anna, and then hand over the estate to her, arranging for her daughter to pay her mother a regular allowance. Anna, at seventeen, already had a fiancé, Georges Mniszech, a pleasant young man of twenty-two, who had a large estate of his own in the western part of the Ukraine. Accordingly, at the end of April 1845, Balzac travelled to Dresden to help Eveline make a decision about her future son-in-law. Fortunately, all four found that they got on very well with each other, and mother, daughter and spouse were highly entertained by Balzac's clowning around.

It is interesting to note that, when the couple were apart, Balzac spent almost as much time writing letters to Eveline as writing novels. As a result there are many unfinished novels left from this period. Not that unfinished works are uncommon from other periods of Balzac's life, but at this time much of his energy was being channelled into establishing his new home with Eveline. She and her daughter finally managed to organise their secret visit to Paris in July 1845, and with them staying in a rented apartment near his house in Passy, Balzac was able to devote much more time again to writing. Eveline and Anna spent a lot of money on fashionable clothes and going to the theatre, while Honoré was able to work away at his antidote to the romantic view of marriage, *Petites Misères de la Vie Conjugale* (to be published in 1846). For him, marriage in his contemporary world had for the most part become a business arrangement.

At the end of July they set off on a trip to Touraine, and visited some of the châteaux of the Loire valley. Then they went on a journey through Holland and into Belgium collecting antiques, each finally going their separate ways at the end of August. He went back to Paris and she to Baden-Baden, but he soon rejoined her there for a week. After returning to Paris again on 5th October, Balzac set off yet again on the 23rd to Chalon-sur-Saône, to be together with Eveline, Anna and Georges. They then spent two weeks sailing from Toulon to Naples. Balzac left them to spend the winter there while he travelled by ship back up the coast of Italy, stopping for some time in Pisa, and spending a lot of money buying antiques in Marseille, before arriving back in Paris on 17th November.

Four months later, Balzac went back to Italy to meet up with Eveline in Rome, where he had an audience with the Pope in April 1846. He asked the Pope to bless a rosary for his mother. They subsequently went back across the Alps and visited, amongst other places, Geneva, Basel and Berne. They went on through Germany to Heidelberg where they parted. By 28th May Balzac was in Passy again. After a thorough period of rest he left six days later for Tours. He stayed in Saché for a week, where he considered buying the beautiful old Château de Moncontour, to use as a country retreat, but Eveline was not willing to finance this little dream. Nevertheless, the visit was fruitful in another respect: he developed ideas for two of his last major works: *La Cousine Bette* and *Le Cousin Pons*. They were to become known under the joint title *Les Parents Pauvres*.

La Cousine Bette was written very much under the influence of the style of the popular serial novel, especially through its use of suspense and frequent changes of pace and sudden twists. It tells the story of the Hulots, who had risen in society under Napoleon, but find themselves ill at ease in the material values of the middle-class Paris of the 1840s. The poor relation, Bette, eventually brings about their downfall.

There is also evidence that Balzac was indulging himself ever more at this time in his long time passion of collecting antiques. He collected objects not only out of fascination with their beauty but also as a financial investment, with the aim of selling many of them again at a profit. The names of several antiques dealers were added to his list of creditors. His obsession with antiques is not unrelated to his detailed depiction of interiors in the novels. In the same period he was becoming more interested in superstitious beliefs, such as palmistry, and he started to suspect that there was significance in the smallest coincidences, such as when a tooth fell out at the same time of day and while eating the same food as when a similar incident had occurred during his stay in St Petersburg. Was it a sign that Eveline was unwell or in danger?[12]

Related or not to these fears, Balzac also learned during 1846 that Eveline was pregnant. Conception, it seems, must have taken place when they were staying in a hotel in Solothurn, in Switzerland. Balzac quickly decided that it would be a boy, and that he would be called Victor-Honoré. He felt convinced that Eveline would now want them to get married as soon as possible. She was staying in Leipzig, in Germany, at the time, and Balzac managed to visit her there once in September. He was hoping to arrange a marriage as soon as possible, but Eveline put him off yet again. In the meantime, her daughter Anna and Georges married in October of that year in Wiesbaden. On 1st

December, however, Balzac received depressing news: Eveline had had a miscarriage. The child, it appeared, would have been a girl. He gained some solace from preparing the small house he had selected for their conjugal bliss in the Rue Fortunée in Paris. It was an old house built before the Revolution, with a narrow garden and the unusual feature of a door leading from the bedroom directly into the nearby Chapelle Saint-Nicolas. It was quite plain on the outside but he had great plans for the interior. All sorts of expensive furnishings and fittings were ordered from all over Europe: mirrors, candelabra, Chinese and Sèvres vases, paintings and engravings. Eveline herself would eventually have to foot the bill in 1850. Perhaps out of concern for his excessive spending, Eveline wrote to him in January 1841, that she would come to Paris.

On 4th February 1847, Balzac went off to Frankfurt, from where he was to fetch Eveline. On arrival in Paris, she stayed first in an apartment in the Rue de Neuve-de-Berry, near the Champs Élysées. That spring proved to be a period of great success for Balzac. His novel *La Cousine Bette* was received with great acclaim, and three other works by him were being serialised in three different newspapers: *Le Député d'Arcis* (never finished) in *L'Union Monarchique*; *La Dernière Incarnation de Vautrin* in *La Presse*; and *Le Cousin Pons* in *Le Constitutionnel*. Some of his pieces about Paris were also published together in this year under the collective title *Les Comèdiens Sans le Savoir*, and for this he wrote a foreword in the third person about himself, praising his own accomplishments with obvious delight and pride. He compared himself, as an equal, to the dramatist Molière.

Early in May, Eveline set off again to attend to affairs in her Russian estate. Balzac accompanied her as far as Frankfurt, before returning to Paris again. Financial problems continued to dog him, not helped by his continuing expenditure on their dream home, and health problems started to plague him again: pains in his ankles, legs and stomach. In the middle of August (the 14th) he went by train to L'Isle d'Adam. It was a journey into memory: he visited again his old haunts in the period when he stayed there with Villers-La-Faye, his father's old friend. Walking around the countryside he had loved so much, he felt little emotion. Unfortunately, it reminded him of how he had been dominated by his mother at the time. He still owed her a tidy sum, though it was not much compared to his other debts. In June he had arranged in his will for Eveline to pay his mother a mere three thousand francs a year after his death. For himself he required only the cheapest of burials.

Before he finally set off to join Eveline at her estate in Wierzchownia, Balzac also made arrangements to help his housekeeper, Louise Breugniot. He tried to find her a job, gave her some of his furniture and also only part of the 10,000 francs which he owed her. There is some evidence, though not conclusive, of Louise Breugniot having attempted to blackmail Balzac. This could, however, have been a rather hysterical show put on to make Eveline jealous. The story is that she stole several letters to Balzac from Eveline and demanded payment of 30,000 francs together with an apology, in writing, for the way in which he had treated her over the years. If this is true, it seems that she was the jealous one. Whatever the truth of the matter, Balzac decided to burn all the letters he had received from Eveline, presumably out of fear that they might fall into unscrupulous hands. He described it as the saddest day of his life, and he managed to save only a few scraps as mementoes from the flames.

On 5th September 1847, Balzac finally set off for Russia. He recorded details of his journey to Wierzchownia in an unpublished travelogue entitled *Lettre sur Kiev* (which actually contains little information about that city). He arrived in Brussels on the morning of the 6th, and had to cross to the other side of the city to catch the train to Cologne. He was helped in his travel arrangements and language difficulties by the family of a Russian *chargé d'affaires* called Kisseleff, which he met en route. Once they had parted in Cologne, however, he was left to his own devices again. The journey continued by coach, with a minor crisis occurring in Breslau when Balzac's luggage was loaded onto the wrong train. Further help concerning travel arrangements came from an encounter with a doctor who was attached to the Austrian Embassy. With this help Balzac travelled to Galicia, where the peasants were living in dire poverty: it was estimated that 60,000 of them had starved to death. The experience led Balzac to express forcefully his preference for rule by benign autocracy.

At the Russian border crossing of Radziwillow, the customs official found that he had run out of the relevant forms and would not let Balzac cross. The dilemma was resolved by the intervention of one General Hackel, who also provided him with an uncomfortable sledge pulled at breakneck speed by one horse. Despite the discomfort, Balzac did enjoy the scenery: from Dubno to Annapol he saw endless fields of wheat with only occasional dwellings. At Berdichev the high road ended. His account of this area reveals a distinct dislike for the Jewish community, which was not uncommon among his contemporaries. From here he only had to travel forty miles through the Ukraine to Wierzchownia. The whole journey took him eight days and he arrived ten days before the actual letter from him which announced his arrival. The community was in the grip of an epidemic of cholera and he had, whether he wished it or not, to stay there throughout the winter.

For a brief period, Balzac enjoyed the experience of domestic bliss, sharing in household activities with Eveline, Anna and Georges, having long talks, doing some reading but not much writing. He described the idyll in his letters to Laure, though he did point out to her that many of the facilities on the estate were inadequate. He stayed there for four and a half months. During this time the only things he wrote were the unfinished *Lettre sur Kiev*, a few other unfinished pieces, and the second part of *L'Envers de l'Histoire Contemporaine* entitled *L'Initié*. It tells of Vanda, the invalid daughter of a Polish woman, who lives under the illusion that she enjoys a luxurious lifestyle, but in fact her father has sold all his treasured books and has furnished one room, her room, in their rundown dwelling, with valuable and expensive items. This work may well have been inspired by a book that Balzac read while he was still in Paris: Charles Dickens' *The Cricket on the Hearth*, in which a man keeps his blind daughter in a fantasy world to shield her from cruel realities.

Finally, at the end of January 1848, Balzac set off again back to Paris, not at all happy at the prospect. He arrived back in Passy on 15th February, and again, not helped by the travails of the journey, his health took a turn for the worse. Unexpected political events were also to affect his plans for the future. On 22nd February, the National Guard were summoned to put down a demonstration organised by two leftwing newspapers, but the guardsmen decided to support the protestors. The army fired on the gathering crowd, and on the 24th, Louis-Philippe abdicated. On the 26th a republic was declared by the provisional government. Balzac was concerned to protect his property but also about the future of the publishing business in the new political climate. He lamented the fact that, because the new regime had changed the whole style of the newspapers, there would probably be no more opportunities for writers of his kind: serial novels were not encouraged. The state of general anarchy that now prevailed persuaded him even more forcibly that he was right in his monarchist views. Publicly, however, he was concerned to be acceptable to the new republic. When he was invited by the Club de la Fraternité Universelle, a revolutionary body, to stand for election, he sent an open letter to the newspapers expressing his support for the establishment of a new empire, and stressed that the plays he was now planning to write would contribute to the development of the new republic. In letters to Eveline and in other unpublished writings, however, he ridiculed many of the republicans' aspirations. Balzac sought out the poet Alphonse de Lamartine, who had now become a political leader, ostensibly showing his support, but also to get his help in acquiring a passport to Russia. The Russians were anxious about the unruly political situation not only in France but also in the rest of Europe, and were not admitting any Frenchmen they considered dubious.

In the meantime, Balzac set about writing the plays that he had been promising everyone. He only managed to complete two. One was *La Marâtre*, about a mother and stepdaughter who are in love with the same man, the whole tragic situation culminating in a suicide. It had its premiere on 25th May 1848, but while the first night was successful, the theatre was half empty because of public fears about the political situation. It closed after six performances. The other play was the comedy, *Mercadet*, of which a draft had already been in existence since 1840. The man Mercadet is waiting for the return of a business associate who went off abroad with 150,000 francs of his money: the man never returns. It is a remarkable coincidence that the thief's name, Godeau, is a homonym of the name of that other famous character in drama who never appears, Godot, in *Waiting for Godot*, by Samuel Beckett. It is very difficult not to credit Beckett with some knowledge of Balzac's dramatic works. *Mercadet* was not so successful as *La Marâtre*, though it was accepted by the Comédie Française, which now sported the politically correct title of the Théâtre de la République. No performance was possible before Balzac went off to Russia, and after that other playwrights managed to get their plays produced instead. It was not performed until a year after Balzac's death.

In June 1848, a counter-revolution took place, and in the elections arranged for December the nephew of Napoleon, Louis Napoleon Bonaparte, became President. Several years later he would be proclaimed Emperor Napoleon III. During the period of the counter-revolution Balzac was safely in Saché, but his health was failing him again. There were frequent palpitations and his eyesight was getting weak. He left Saché on 4th July, reaching his house in Rue Fortunée on the evening of 6th July. He prepared for his eventual departure again for Russia, arranging for his mother to take care of the house and Laurent-Jan to handle his literary affairs. Finally, on 20th August, he received the news he had been waiting for: he had been granted the passport and the Russians were letting him in. On 20th September Balzac left for Russia.

He arrived at Wierzchownia on 2nd October 1848. Here he led a settled and sure existence, respected and liked by the local people and servants, as if he were a kind old member of the landed gentry. Meanwhile, in his absence from Paris, his name was put forward in January 1849, for election to the Académie Française. Although Lamartine and Victor Hugo supported him, Balzac did not receive a sufficient number of votes. It was clearly no great disappointment to him, as many other famous writers had not been awarded the honour.

Despite the apparent realisation of his dream existence in Wierzchownia, there were still several reasons for postponing actual marriage. Prominent among these were a series of local natural disasters: a hailstorm followed by some kind of blight ruined the harvest in 1849. Then the estate's mill was destroyed by lightning, and fires broke out in the sheep-pens and the wheat fields. Also, many hundreds of peasants in the region were homeless and beginning to make their demands for housing very vocal. This all meant an enormous drain on Eveline's financial resources. To add to their woes, it was confirmed in July of that year that Eveline would lose the estate if she married Balzac. Despite all these setbacks, Balzac stayed on. He was still there in February 1850. He wrote to his mother with one excuse after another: the weather, marauding bandits, etc. The main problem, however, was the continuing decline in his health.

It is impossible to provide a precise description of Balzac's medical condition, but most of the doctors who examined him were in agreement about one major problem: cardiac hypertrophy, or swelling of the heart. The causes could be and probably were manifold, and his condition was undoubtedly aggravated by the lifestyle he had maintained over the years, frequently working for long stretches without sleep and stimulating himself with far too much coffee. In the last eighteen months or so of his life the symptoms of Balzac's general decline were unpleasant and varied: peritonitis, gastric fever, bronchitis, difficulties in breathing and loss of energy, to name but a few. In June 1849, he wrote to Laure complaining about hallucinations, vomiting and dizziness. In October, he developed a fever which lasted over a month, and there were signs of dropsy. Then in January 1850, he had to take to his bed again for ten days. Despite all this, Balzac was determined to keep as mobile as possible, and at the end of this month he went with Eveline to attend a fair in Kiev. This led to him having to lie in a hotel bed for about twenty days with symptoms resembling a cold.

It was at this stage that Eveline finally consented to marry him.

There has been much speculation about why Eveline suddenly made her mind up within a matter of months of his death. Was it out of material interest? This argument is hardly tenable, as she was thereby ceding ownership of the estate to her daughter. A generous interpretation of her motives seems more justified: they both sensed that he might not have much longer to live, and she wanted to fulfil Balzac's dearest wish. The ceremony was held in the parish church of St Barbara's in Berdichev on the morning of 14th March 1850. They travelled back to Wierzchownia the same day, arriving at half-past ten in the evening. Both were exhausted, and Eveline took to her bed with arthritic pains and rheumatic aches.

By late April they had decided to make their way back to Paris, and they set off on the 24th, passing through Brody, in the Austrian part of Galicia, Radziwillow, and arriving in Dresden on 9th May, where they managed to put in a little browsing in the shops. They arrived back in Paris just in time to celebrate Balzac's fifty-first birthday on 20th May. Balzac had travelled for two days without eating anything or sleeping. He could not see clearly and frequently lapsed into unconsciousness. The first problem they had to deal with was to care for Balzac's servant, who, left alone in the house for so long, had, for whatever reasons, become deranged. He had to be taken off to an asylum.

Balzac managed to be fairly active for a while, dealing with the arrival of goods and valuable items that had been sent to the Paris address. But from the beginning of June he became bedridden. By the middle of July he had become too weak even to dictate letters. Various doctors were called in to treat his symptoms. He was bled, purged and had a hundred leeches put on his stomach. Mouth ulcers, blisters and bedsores proliferated. Still somehow he managed to keep cheerful and even joke about the prospect of death. His condition now became widely known, and, amongst others, Victor Hugo came to visit him.

Rumours spread after Balzac's death which even now occupy biographers and critics, that Eveline was unfaithful to him in his last days. As with many other mysteries in Balzac's life, however, the evidence is not conclusive either way. The story was that a certain painter named Jean Gigoux, who is known to have had an affair with Eveline after Balzac's death, was actually providing her with a little more than just consolation while Balzac was dying. It is certain that Eveline became familiar with Gigoux during 1851 when he was painting a portrait of Anna. At the time when Balzac was dying Gigoux was actually having an affair with the wife of another painter, who lived next door to the Balzacs. Both Balzac's sister, Laure, and Zulma Carraud later claimed that the relationship between Honoré and Eveline was not without some turbulence in his final days. These are the bare bones of the facts, and the rest is speculation or hearsay. It is, after all, not unlikely that there were some moments of stress, when one partner was suffering excruciating discomfort: illness does tend to make one oversensitive and irritable. In his last dictated letter, to his business adviser, August Fessart, Balzac mentions how his wife was beginning to find it difficult with his illness but that he was thankful for the enormous happiness his marriage had brought him.[13] These are hardly the words of an embittered man.

By 17th August the doctors recognised that gangrene had set in, and that there was nothing more they could do. By the morning Balzac could no longer speak nor see, and the priest from the chapel of Saint-Philippe-du-Roule next door was summoned to give him the last sacraments. Balzac was able to indicate that he understood what was happening. That evening Victor Hugo came again for a final visit, but left again before the end. On 18th August 1850, at half-past eleven in the evening, Honoré de Balzac died.

Eveline lived together with her husband's mother for some time. They never got on well, and after several months his mother left to live with a friend. She died in 1854. Eveline stayed on in the house, large parts of which were closed off and left to gather dust. Her son-in-law went insane and died in 1881, and the house had to be sold in 1882, because she and her daughter could no longer afford the upkeep. Eveline was, however, allowed to continue living there until she died, on 11th April 1882, at the probable age of seventy-six. Anna went into a convent, where she died childless in 1915.

The Legacy

Attitudes to Balzac have always been mixed, both towards his literary creations and his personal life: he was an unruly, disorganised genius, or he was just unruly and disorganised; he provided inspired insights into an entire society, or he was obsessed with cataloguing its vices and depravities. It was felt by many contemporaries that the reading of his works had led many a young man into a life of self-seeking materialism. But there were those who recognised his greatness.

Writing in 1858, Hippolyte Taine admired the Naturalist and visionary qualities of Balzac's writing, considering his works as a whole, a storehouse of information about human nature.[14] Victor Hugo, in his funeral oration, idealised Balzac as a revolutionary writer despite his demonstrably conservative tendencies.[15] And Émile Zola, in his *Le Roman Expérimental* (1880), considered Balzac to be essentially an experimental scientist and the father of Naturalism in literature.[16] While recognising Balzac's greatness as an observer of human nature, Charles Baudelaire, in his essay of 1859, agreed with Taine in finding that Balzac's principal achievement was as a visionary.

Despite these positive evaluations by some of his contemporaries, however, Balzac's popularity with the reading public was outshone during the twenty-five years or so after his death by that of other contemporaries, such as Alexandre Dumas the older, Eugène Sue and George Sand. *La Comédie humaine* was for a long time considered to be not very respectable reading. But with the publication from 1894 of his letters to Eveline Hanska, *Lettres à l'Étrangère*, Balzac came to be viewed in the public imagination as something of a romantic hero.

Other writers known to have been influenced by him are Fyodor Dostoevsky, who, at the age of twenty-two, translated *Eugénie Grandet* into Russian, and Gustave Flaubert. There were few positive responses from British writers in the nineteenth and early twentieth century. Both George Eliot and Charlotte Brontë found Balzac's books distasteful,[17] and Lytton Strachey found him coarse.[18] Elizabeth Barrett Browning was one of the few to show enthusiasm.[19] Outside literature, Karl Marx praised his grasp of social realities in *Das Kapital*. Other writers who began to sing his praises were Oscar Wilde, Algernon Charles Swinburne and Henry James.

In his essay on Balzac, published in *Notes on Novelists with Some Other Notes* (1914), Henry James praises Balzac highly while not being unaware of the problems caused by the enormity of the task the author had imposed on himself. On the one hand James can describe him as 'the first and foremost member of his craft', but then a few pages later he admits that the reader is often 'unable to see the wood for the trees'. His greatest strength is the obverse of his greatest weakness: 'This identity of his universal with his local and national vision is the particular thing we should doubtless call his greatest strength were we preparing agreeably to speak of it also as his visible weakness.' The paradox of this greatness is the result of a dual ambition: 'the artist of the *Comédie humaine* is half smothered by the historian'. Though his praise may be qualified, James finally stands in awe of Balzac's achievement: 'One really knows in all imaginative literature no undertaking to compare with it for courage, good faith and sublimity.'[20]

In the twentieth century, broadly conceived Marxist criticism, as exemplified by Walter Benjamin and Georg Lukacs, also perceived Balzac as the progenitor of Modernist modes of thought.

Two renowned biographers, Stefan Zweig and André Maurois, literary giants in their own right, also devoted extensive studies to him. For Zweig Balzac was 'endowed with an exuberance of imagination which puts it in his power to establish and populate a universe of his own creation'.[21] Maurois also saw Balzac as a Promethean figure who had stolen the power to create from the gods themselves and embodied a universe: 'No writer other than Shakespeare has been the object of so much study, or has more deserved to be. Balzac has been explored, and will continue to be explored, like a world, because that is what he is.'[22] In his foreword to a German edition of Balzac's story 'La Fille aux Yeux d'Or', Hugo von Hofmannsthal, renowned as a lyric poet and for his libretti for operas by Richard Strauss, wrote: 'I do not know of any desire which might dwell in the imagination of a reader which would not be satisfied by the books of this man.'[23]

Marcel Proust clearly had mixed feelings about Balzac. In an essay, to be found in a continuous form in his notebooks, Proust is critical of Balzac's obsessive need to explain everything: 'And when there is an explanation to be given, he does not hold back'; 'Similarly, he has summaries in which he states everything we ought to know, allowing us no room to breathe or to move.' On the other hand, Proust recognises the subtlety with which Balzac reveals character: 'The same man who exhibits his own historical, artistic, etc., opinions so artlessly, conceals his deeper designs, allowing the truthfulness of his depiction of his characters' language to make its own point, so subtly that it may go unremarked, with no attempt to draw attention to it.'[24] Surely the clearest indication of Proust's respect for Balzac is in his own massive, multi-volume novel, a twentieth-century equivalent of *La Comédie humaine*.

One of the writers who can be said to have matched Balzac with his prolific output is the Belgian author, renowned for his crime fiction though long under-valued as a serious writer, Georges Simenon. He wrote just under 200 novels in his own name and over 200 under eighteen pseudonyms, with many volumes of short stories, several autobiographies and twenty-two volumes of memoirs. In January 1960, he wrote an account of Balzac's life, which was used in a television documentary in the series 'Portrait-Souvenir'. In his dedication to the published version of the text he emphasises that he had not chosen the topic: it had been chosen for him. He adds: 'I do not believe that I have anything in common with the novelist of *La Comédie humaine* except, perhaps, abundance.'[25] In his account, however, Simenon provides some sensitive insights into the forces that drove Balzac to create the multitude of his characters. When he wonders about whether this need to be so prolific could have arisen in a man who was happy with his circumstances, it is difficult not to believe that this conviction was rooted in Simenon's insight into his own nature. Simenon was frequently asked why he wrote so many short novels. When was he going to write some big novels? His reply, in an interview with Carvel Collins, published in 1956, suggests that he saw his entire output as an integrated whole, a concept not so remote from that of *La Comédie humaine*: 'I will never write a big book. My big book is the mosaic of all my small novels.'[26]

In 1950, UNESCO decided to celebrate the centenary of Balzac's death with a special publication, entitled *Hommage à Balzac*. In preparation for this, a letter was sent out to various writers all over the world by the then director general, Jaime Torres, inviting them to write a piece on Balzac. The letter included praise of Balzac's universality, describing his work as popular in the best sense of the word: appealing to readers both refined and unrefined in their taste. The essays to be included in the volume were to reflect these dual aspects of his work: its universality and its popularity. The writers should also indicate the contemporary relevance of the great writer for their countries and the role his work played in the literatures of those countries. There were contributions from France, England, Norway, Spain, Sweden, Poland, etc. In his essay, *Actualité de Balzac*, the French writer and member of the Académie Française, François

Mauriac, stressed how fresh Balzac's style still seemed after a hundred years, despite the 'flamboyant baroque nature of its form', the immensity of his output ('ninety-one works composed in less than twenty years'), the extent to which his words express much more than their apparent meaning, and his incomparable evocation of 'a black universe, one of the most criminal ones ever created by literature'.[27]

In the twentieth century, there have also been numerous adaptations of Balzac's work for film and television. Scarcely was cinema born before directors were drawn to his works. The International Movie Database lists no less than 144 films since 1909, either based on works by, or recounting aspects of the life of, Balzac. The lack of sound did not daunt the early pioneers. The earliest recorded is the 1909 film of *Les Paysans*, with a version of *La Peau de Chagrin* in the same year. Amongst others, versions of *Le Père Goriot* and *Eugénie Grandet* appeared in 1910. Italian and Swedish films of his works were appearing by 1916, and German versions from 1918 onwards. In fact barely a year passes after that when there was not at least one screen adaptation of a Balzac work in one language or other, with TV versions appearing from the 1950s onwards. In 1960, Sergei Alekseyev directed a Russian film, recognisable from its transliterated title, *Evgeniya Grande*. More recently, Gérard Depardieu appeared as Colonel Chabert in a 1994 film, and in 1999 he appeared as Balzac himself in a TV dramatisation of the author's life. Finally, as an indication of how widely Balzac's influence has travelled and how his work has, for some, come to speak directly to the hearts of people from completely different cultural backgrounds, there is the example of the success of the novel *Balzac and the Little Chinese Seamstress*, adapted and directed as a film from her own novel by Dai Sijiie, under the Chinese title *Xiao cai feng* (2002). The film tells of how, in 1971, two young students are sent to a mountain village in China for re-education during the Cultural Revolution. They attempt to woo a charming young seamstress with a secret cache of forbidden western literature, which includes works by Balzac. In the process of teaching the girl, the youths themselves learn what a powerful force literature can be.

The sheer immensity of Balzac's achievement has been summed up well by two men who greatly admired him: Victor Hugo in his funeral eulogy and André Maurois near the end of his biography. The intensity with which Balzac lived his life was emphasised by Hugo: '

> His life was short, but it was full. It was richer in works than in days. Alas! This tremendous, unwearying worker, this philosopher, this thinker, this poet, this genius, experienced during his sojourn among us that life full of storms and struggles which is the lot of all great men.[28]

How he transmuted the sufferings of that life into art was what fascinated Maurois above all:

> From the day when Honoré de Balzac set out to give to the world, transforming them in the process, the stern, chilly gaze of his mother, the sorrows of his neglected childhood, his reading under the stairs at Vendôme, his first 'scent of woman', the vicissitudes of his brother-in-law, the squalid stratagems of usurers, his lost illusions and his creative ecstasy, he sustained a multitude of living people with his own substance.[29]

Notes

1. Honoré de Balzac, *Entre Savants*, from *La Comédie humaine*, vol XII, p. 541.

2. Laure Surville, 1858, p. 21.

3. Edouard Monnais, 1850.

4. Balzac, *Correspondance*, vol I, p. 36.

5. George Sand, 1971, vol II, p. 155.

6. Balzac, *The Wild Ass's Skin*, 1977, p. 52.

7. Balzac, *The Unknown Masterpiece*, 2001, p. 40.

8. Balzac, *History of the Thirteen*, 1974, p. 21.

9. Albéric Second, 1886, p. 7.

10. Balzac, *Lettres à Mme. Hanska*, vol I, p. 145.

11. Graham Robb, 2000, p. 357.

12. Balzac, *Lettres à Mme. Hanska*, vol I, p. 940.

13. Balzac, *Correspondance*, vol V, pp. 795–6.

14. Hippolyte Taine, 1858.

15. Victor Hugo, 1985.

16. Émile Zola, 1880.

17. D. Adamson, 1992, pp. 391–420.

18. Lytton Strachey, 1943, p. 225.

19. Elizabeth Barrett Browning and Robert Browning, 1984–1891, vol VIII, p. 316.

20. Henry James, 1948, pp. 24, 27, 26, 24 and 40, respectively.

21. Stefan Zweig, 1946, p. 3.

22. André Maurois, 1983, p. 11.

23. Hugo von Hofmannsthal, 1961, p. 5 [text here translated by the present author].

24. Marcel Proust, 1988, pp. 63 and 64, respectively.

25. Georges Simenon, 1960, p. 21 [here translated by the present author].

26. Simenon, 1956, p. 90.

27. François Mauriac, 1950, pp. 322, 325 and 336 respectively [here translated by the present author].

28. Quoted in Zweig, 1946, p. 387.

29. Maurois, 1965, p. 560.

Chronological list of works

This chronology is approximate due to the complexity of Balzac's writing and publication history. The titles given below are the final ones used by Balzac. Lesser-known works, including journalism and plays, are not included. The first three works were published under pseudonyms. Details of all Balzac's works and indications of how Balzac organised his prose fiction in his scheme for *La Comédie humaine*, can be found in Graham Robb's biography.

1822 *Le Centenaire*
    Le Vicaire des Ardennes
1826 *Wann-Chlore*
1829 *Les Chouans*
    La Physiologie du Mariage
1830 *Gobseck*
    La Maison du chat qui pelote
1831 *La Peau de Chagrin*
    'Le Chef d'oeuvre Inconnu'
1832 *Le Colonel Chabert*
    Le Curé de Tours
    Louis Lambert
    Les Contes Drolatiques (the first ten only)
1833 *Le Médecin de Campagne*
    'La Grenadière'
    'L'Illustre Gaudissart'
    Eugénie Grandet
1834 *La Recherche de l'Absolu*
    Histoire des Treize
1835 *Le Père Goriot*
1836 *Le Lys dans la Vallée*
    'Facino Cane'
1837 *Illusions Perdues* (first part)
    César Birotteau
1838 *La Torpille* (first part of *Splendeurs et Misères des Courtisanes*)
1839 'Gambara'
    'Les Secrets de la Princesse de Cadignan'
    Illusions Perdues (second part)
1840 'Pierre Grassou'
    'Z. Marcas'

1841 'Le Curé de Village'
1842 'Ursule Mirouët'
La Rabouilleuse
1843 *Une Ténébreuse Affaire*
Illusions Perdues (complete work in three parts)
1844 'Modeste Mignon'
'Béatrix'
1846 *L'Envers de l'Histoire Contemporaine* (first episode)
La Cousine Bette
1847 *Le Cousin Pons*
Splendeurs et Misères des Courtisanes (complete work)
1848 *L'Initié* (second episode of *L'Envers de l'Histoire Contemporaine*)

Select Bibliography

Adamson, D., 'La Réception de *La Comédie humaine* en Grande Bretagne au XXe siècle', in *L'Année Balzacienne* (Paris, 1992).

Balzac, Honoré de, *Correspondance*, ed. Roger Pierrot (Paris, 1960–9) vol I;

— *History of the Thirteen*, tr. Herbert J. Hunt (Harmondsworth, 1974);

— *La Comédie humaine* (Paris, 1976–1981);

— *The Wild Ass's Skin*, tr. Herbert J. Hunt (Harmondsworth, 1977);

— *Lettres à Madame Hanska*, ed. Roger Pierrot (Paris, 1990), vol I;

— *The Unknown Masterpiece*, tr. Richard Howard (New York, 2001).

Bardèche, Maurice, *Balzac* (Paris, 1980).

Browning, Elizabeth Barrett and Robert, *The Brownings' Correspondence*, eds P. Kelley, R. Hudson and S. Lewis (Winfield, KS, 1984–91), vol VIII.

Citron, Pierre, *Dans Balzac* (Paris, 1986).

Hofmannsthal, Hugo von, Foreword to *Das Mädchen mit den Goldaugen* (German translation of Balzac, H de, *La Fille aux Yeux d'Or*) (Frankfurt am Main, 1961).

Hugo, Victor, 'Discours prononcé aux funérailles de M. Honoré de Balzac' in *Actes et Paroles. I. Avant L'Exil, 1841–1851* (Paris, 1985).

James, Henry, 'Honoré de Balzac' in 'Notes on Novelists with Some Other Notes' (1914), included in *The Art of Fiction and Other Essays* (New York, 1948).

Mauriac, François, 'Actualité de Balzac', in *Hommage à Balzac* (Paris, 1950).

Maurois, André, *Prometheus: The Life of Balzac*, translated by Norman Denny (New York, 1965; 1989).

Monnais, Edouard ('E.M.'), 'Honoré de Balzac', in *Revue et Gazette Musicale* (Paris, 1st September 1850).

Pierrot, Roger, *Honoré de Balzac* (Paris, 1994).

Proust, Marcel, 'Saint-Beuve and Balzac' in *Against Sainte-Beuve and Other Essays* (London, 1988).

Robb, Graham. *Balzac*, (London, 1994; 2000).

Sand, George, *Histoire de ma Vie*, in *Oeuvres Autobiographiques* (Paris, 1971), vol II.

Second, Albéric, *Le Tiroir aux Souvenirs* (Paris, 1886).

Simenon, Georges, 'Georges Simenon, An Interview on the Art of Fiction', conducted by Carvel Collins, in *Publications in the Humanities Number 23*, Cambridge MA, 1956;

— *Portrait-Souvenir de Balzac, et autres textes sur la literature*, Christian Bourgois (France, 1960).

Sipriot, Pierre, *Balzac sans masque*, (Paris, 1992).

Strachey, Lytton, *Landmarks in French Literature* (Oxford, 1912; 1943).

Surville, Laure, *Balzac, sa vie et ses oeuvres d'après sa correspondance* (Paris, 1858).

Taine, Hippolyte, 'Balzac', in *Journal des Débats* (Paris, February and March 1858).

Troyat, Henri, *Balzac* (Paris, 1995).

Zola, Émile, *Le Roman Expérimental* (Paris, 1880).

Zweig, Stefan, *Balzac*, translated by William and Dorothy Rose (New York, 1946).

SELECTED TITLES FROM HESPERUS PRESS

Brief Lives

Author	Title
Richard Canning	*Brief Lives: Oscar Wilde*
Gavin Griffiths	*Brief Lives: Joseph Conrad*
Patrick Miles	*Brief Lives: Anton Chekhov*
Fiona Stafford	*Brief Lives: Jane Austen*
Melissa Valiska Gregory and Melisa Klimaszewski	*Brief Lives: Charles Dickens*

Classics, Modern Voices and New Fiction

Author	Title	Foreword writer
Honoré de Balzac	*Colonel Chabert*	A.N. Wilson
Honoré de Balzac	*Sarrasine*	Kate Pullinger
Honoré de Balzac	*The Vendetta*	
Charles Baudelaire	*On Wine and Hashish*	Margaret Drabble
Cyrano de Bergerac	*Journey to the Moon*	Andrew Smith
Alexandre Dumas	*The Corsican Brothers*	Frank Wynne
Gustave Flaubert	*Memoirs of a Madman*	Germaine Greer
Gustave Flaubert	*November*	Nadine Gordimer
Laurent Gaudé	*The Scortas' Sun*	
Yasmine Ghata	*The Calligraphers' Night*	
Joris-Karl Huysmans	*With the Flow*	Simon Callow
Guy de Maupassant	*Butterball*	Germaine Greer
Prosper Mérimée	*Carmen*	Philip Pullman
Antoine François Prévost	*Manon Lescaut*	Germaine Greer
Marcel Proust	*Pleasures and Days*	A.N. Wilson
Marquis de Sade	*Incest*	Janet Street-Porter
Stendhal	*Memoirs of an Egotist*	Doris Lessing
Stendhal	*Letters to Pauline*	Adam Thirlwell
Emile Zola	*For a Night of Love*	A.N. Wilson
Emile Zola	*The Dream*	Tim Parks

Biographical note

Dr David Carter has taught at St Andrews and Southampton universities in the UK and is presently Professor of Communicative English at Yonsei University, Seoul. He has published on psychoanalysis, literature, drama, film history and applied linguistics, and is also a freelance journalist and translator. He has published books on the Belgian author *Georges Simenon* and *Literary Theory*, as well as in the field of film studies, the most recent being *East Asian Cinema* and *The Western*. For Hesperus he has translated Georges Simenon's *Three Crimes,* Honoré de Balzac's 'Sarrasine' and Klaus Mann's *Alexander*.